The Complete Mountain Biker

The Complete Mountain Biker

Dennis Coello

L&B

Lyons & Burford
Publishers

for ART

Printed in the United States of America

10 9 8 7 6 5 4 3 2

Library of Congress Cataloging-in-Publication Data

Coello, Dennis.
    The complete mountain biker / Dennis Coello.
      p.   cm.
    Includes index.
    ISBN 1-55821-021-0 : $12.95
      1. All terrain cycling. 2. All terrain bicycles. I. Title.
GV1043.C58   1989   89-7961
796.6—dc20   CIP

Contents

Acknowledgments

As I stated in *Touring on Two Wheels*, most of my writing is solo, but book production is a *group* endeavor. Many thanks, therefore, to Kris Peterson, Mary Perkins, Dennis Nieweg, and Dave Taff for their artwork, to Shimano for its contribution of mechanical drawings and instructions, to my editor Peter Burford and his entire staff, and to those named and unnamed individuals who appear in the photos and paragraphs that follow.

Introduction

This is a book for beginners. It's short, simple, and filled with pictures—a combination designed *not* to confuse the newcomer. Whether you're brand new to mountain biking and don't know which bike to buy, or wish simply to begin using your wheels for a side of the sport you're unfamiliar with (commuting, trail riding, backcountry touring . . .), or need a thorough maintenance and repair guide to restore the bike you've been mistreating since you bought it—this book is for you.

I've deliberately included many photographs, and relatively little text, a picture being, as they say, worth a thousand words. Take for instance the section on trail-riding skills. I could go on for pages about saddle position during climbs and steep descents, expressing at great length what a series of photos gives the viewer at a glance. Turn to that chapter and you will see a few paragraphs of riding basics, followed by photos with explanatory captions. It's the same in the chapter on bike selection, repairs, accessories, and so on.

A second reason for brevity is that mountain biking is still a very fast-changing sport. By the time a writer gathers his data and publishes it (usually a year or more), much of the detailed technical information is old hat. I write a monthly column for *Mountain Bike Magazine,* as well as feature articles for a half-dozen other cycling journals, and on occasion have difficulty in not appearing dated in their short three-month publication lead-time.

So why a book? Why not simply suggest a thorough reading of the latest mags and a visit to the bike shop? The answer is that newcomers to any field of this sport would be confused by most mountain bike articles, as they are written primarily with the somewhat-experienced rider in mind. And the bike shops? In most you are in very capable, honest hands. But you'll still see only the bikes that particular shop has to offer. And so many facts bombard the novice that he often leaves a shop more confused than informed.

A book devoted to the basics, on the other hand, is easily understood, does not become outdated, and serves as a necessary prerequisite for the graduate courses in mountain biking served up each month in magazines. And all the formerly over-your-head bike shop blather will now make sense.

Drop the few bucks for this book before you buy your bike and you're very likely to prevent the several-hundred-dollar mistake of winding up with a rig you'll be looking to trade within the year. Read over the paragraphs on gearing and tires and you'll ease your way up hills that are impossible on bikes with "stock" equipment. Shave days off your training for rough trails (and save your skull while you're at it) by studying my photos. And avoid long walks back to trailheads, and costly shop repairs, by learning proper maintenance procedure.

Inexpensive, easy to read, an introduction to the world of go-almost-anywhere mountain bikes. What a deal.

1

Selecting a Bike

I EARN HALF my living as a photographer, and purchase film in large quantities from mail-order firms in New York. You know the kind of place—the toll-free number is busy the first twenty times you call, a man finally answers in a voice that reminds you of army drill sergeants, and when you hang up you're sure your film will arrive at the wrong address.

Last week I made another call. The disembodied voice on the phone gruffly took my order, demanded my Visa number and expiration date, then asked for the name on the card. I gave it. For the first time in the conversation there was a pause. Then he spoke. "Coello—the biker?" Amazed, I mumbled out an affirmative reply. It brought an immediate response: "Which mountain bike should I buy?"

The fellow's question is memorable for its context, but the query is not at all unique. I've heard those words literally hundreds of times in the past few years, asked by people who are convinced they want an ATB, but haven't the foggiest at how to go about choosing one. So let's start off with the two questions I asked my suddenly friendly New Yorker:

1. What kind of riding do you intend to do?

2. How much money do you have to spend?

Let's deal first with question one. I've found over the years that most people fall roughly into three categories in their answers.

a) those who plan solely to ride to work
b) those who wish to do a bit of everything—commuting/dirt roads/ trails/touring
c) those who envision themselves as two-wheeled skiers (sometimes referred to as "gonzo" or "kamikaze" riders; also referred to occasionally as dead, laid up, not walking so well any longer . . .)

Choosing a category will at least narrow the number of bikes to test ride. But don't be hasty in making a decision, and try, if possible, to ride a borrowed bike or two before making up your mind. Let me give an example of why careful deliberation on this point is important.

Let's say that for whatever reason you have absolutely no desire in riding trails or doing any backcountry touring. But you've read all about the roughly half a buck per driven mile you'll save by riding to work, and want the added advantage of a cross-town aerobic workout instead of a half-asleep drive. (If you're an accountant you have probably already figured that with roughly 220 workdays per year and, say, a fifteen-mile roundtrip ride, you'll save—at fifty cents per mile—a whopping total of $1,650 *annually*.)

Commuters do not require a full-on mountain bike, a point that has

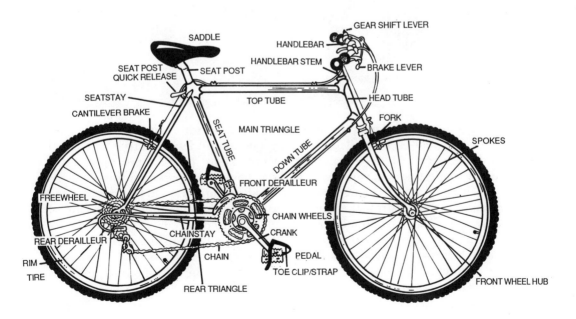

caused several manufacturers to offer "city bikes" with thinner tires, higher gears, and swept-back handlebars. These mounts cost less than true ATBs, and chances are you will be content—for a while. Then you'll happen upon a dirt road or single track (narrow trail), and get hooked on backroad travel.

This may appear a lengthy digression after I promised to be brief. But the reason is simply to stress the need to answer my first question ("What kind of riding do you intend to do?") *very* carefully before proceeding to question two, and especially before purchasing a bike that cannot be transformed for all kinds of travel. In short, buy a city bike and that's exactly what you get. Purchase a true mountain bike, however, and you can redesign the rig for almost any purpose and all terrains.

Most prospective fat-tire bikers fall into category two—those who wish to do all kinds of riding. Knowing this, the bike companies have made your choices difficult by offering an unbelievable array of machines. So for you people, and for the third group of no-holds-barred bikers, the second question of cost is all-important.

What will you get for $350, $500, $700? The answer changes almost each month, depending as it does on dollar-to-yen valuation and supply and demand. There are, however, some very general price categories that will give you a rough idea of what to expect in the shops. I present the following information in this manner because for most buyers *it is all they will want to know before choosing a bike.* It is my experience that newcomers to the sport find that articles and, especially, books present far too much information on frame geometry/composition and similar particulars (expect to be bombarded with head and seat tube angles by salesmen; the drawings and captions should make this understandable). I have therefore listed minimum requirements, provided some particulars to be looked for in each general price range, and added suggestions on choosing the right-sized bike for your body and riding style. Only after these general buying guidelines (again, those which are sufficient for most cyclists), do I enter into those discussions which for most riders are simply esoterica.

$300 to $450

I recently did a review of mountain bikes under $450 for *Outside* Magazine, and found not only that very great differences exist in this price range, but that one does not necessarily get a better bike for a higher price. In other words be careful, and shop around.

At the low end of this range you will find the entry level bikes of heavy steel frames, steel rims, gum tires (rather than the much lighter skinwalls), poor brakes, and unresponsive derailleurs. My strong suggestion is that you live bikeless for a few more months until you can afford a better machine, one that includes these minimum requirements:

1. *lightweight frame*—where at least the main triangle (top, seat, and down tubes) are of chrome-molybdenum (a strong, lightweight alloy). Good-quality, lightweight aluminum frames have been dropping in price of late, but I would be surprised if they will soon be available in this relatively low range. The main point here is to avoid all-steel frames, which produce sluggish performance on any riding surface. Expect lower-priced models to fall into the 30-pound range, most mid-priced bikes to run around 28.

2. *aluminum-alloy rims*—steel rims are much heavier and also harder to stop when wet.

Sealed bearings.

3. *sealed bearings*—"sealed" in most cases actually means simply *more* sealed against the elements than those unsealed hub, bottom bracket, pedal, and head-set bearings still found on many touring bikes. The words become confusing because there are some *truly* sealed hubs which require factory maintenance, or come equipped with grease fittings. A drawback with the sealed bearings commonly found is that they are more difficult for the mechanic (and you) to get into; the benefit is that maintenance is needed far less often because road grit is also denied easy access. (See Chapter Seven for sealed bearing maintenance.)

4. *strong brakes*—"strong" is here defined as sufficient to give you confidence in stopping the bike (to be determined by *you*, not the salesman), after several comparison test rides. My personal preference is the brake found on the early mountain bikes, and now unfortunately present on many models only on the front wheel—the cantilever. Quick, tough, and easy to maintain, my feeling is that manufacturers should have left well enough alone. In recent articles I have criticized some less expensive models of U-brakes (mounted under the chainstays and behind the bottom bracket) for being "mushy." I expect the manufacturers to respond quickly to riders' criticisms, but even with the best of U-brakes their mounting position makes the attachment of a regular kickstand impossible (Mountain Aid Products now offers a U-brake model), and though protective cordura brake covers exist, the location is still bad for dirt, mud, and snow buildup. You will also run into the "roller cam" (or "power cam") brakes

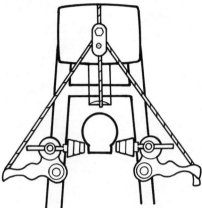

Cantilever brake.

which have great stopping power, but at first were very difficult to adjust. Later models have become easier to work with, and can be kept relatively clean with cordura "cam covers."

There is one last problem with U-brakes that I've not experienced personally (in fact, I've experienced no problems whatsoever from the two bikes I ride which sport high-quality U-brakes), but have heard about from friends. In all cases the riders who told me of the problem had seen the effects firsthand—a deep wear point on the tire sidewall from the brake pad. Due to the U-brake configuration worn pads are drawn up and in upon the tire sidewall, whereas cantilever pads move further down upon the metal rim. It is one more reason for me to hope that the industry moves away from U-brakes, and a good reminder to those of us who buy them to make frequent maintenance checks. In two of the three cases mentioned above the rear tires were damaged beyond repair.

5. *bottom bracket*—ATB bottom brackets must be higher than those found on touring bikes, to clear obstacles and allow pedaling around tight turns on trails. The heights of different brands vary, so compare them to other mountain and touring bikes.

Roller cam brake.

Index shift lever.

6. *indexed shifting*(?)—the question mark is added because many riders these days apparently feel indexed or "click" shifting (the changing of gears through the pushing of one's handlebar derailleur shifter in one direction or another until a click is heard) is a must. Racers and hard trail bikers are especially fond of the newer designs from SunTour and Shimano's Hyperglide system that allow maximum-load indexed shifting of the rear derailleur across seven-sprocket freewheels. I still prefer the feel of the old-style "friction" shifters, and have found that indexed systems require more care to keep them working well. Fortunately, all click shifters also have an optional friction mode.

7. *multi-piece, five "pin" cotterless crankset*—I don't know of any mountain bikes which use cotter pins to fix the crankarms to the spindle (bottom bracket axle); nor have I seen any ATBs with one-piece cranksets and only three "pins" radiating out to the chainrings. (Cotter-pin attachment makes the servicing of bottom bracket bearings a nightmare; multi-piece cranks allow for the easy and comparatively inexpensive changing of chainrings; five pins—in place of three—help keep the crankset "true"—revolving in a straight line, thereby not slapping the chain against the front derailleur cage.) But my not having seen bikes with these drawbacks does not insure you against running into them. Be wary.

So much for "minimum requirements." There are plenty of other *preferences* which I could name (and will in the next price category), but most of these can be obtained through inexpensive upgrades after purchase. Let me add, however, that in my tests of a dozen or so bikes up to the $450 cutoff I did not find a single bike with the kind of wide, dual-purpose skinwall tires that truly ease one's travel in both the paved and unpaved worlds. (My favorite by far—the Crossroads II, 1.95″ wide interlocking knobbies, 35–80 psi.) Most common were relatively low-pressure, thin (1.62″ usually) tires—too soft for fast pavement travel, too thin for good traction in dirt. Saddles also left much to be desired. The frames of almost all bikes in this range were produced in Taiwan, where manufacturing standards are supposedly somewhat lower (though this appears to be changing) than those built in Japan. Frame flex—where forward-movement pedal power is diminished by lateral sway (noticeable to very experienced riders while in the saddle, but often tested for by standing next to the bike, placing a foot on the pedal while at the six-o'clock position and pushing downward), and slight pinholes at weld points showed up in some of the bikes I tested. But neither "problem" would even be noticed by most riders.

Choose carefully in the upper end of this price bracket, upgrade tires and expand the gear range (as discussed below), and you will have a bike that's great in town and on dirt roads, and good on trails. You will be pushing perhaps two or so pounds more than with bikes in the next category, and have to put up with components which do not have the crisp, sharp feel of the more expensive derailleurs, brakes, and so on.

$450 to $700

Most riders who drop this much money on an ATB will never have to buy a "better" bike. That is, no matter their pleasure—year-round and year-long commuting, loaded touring, tough trails—these bikes generally will handle the abuse. I say "generally" to caution you still to buy with care, comparing the frames, component groups, tires, gear ranges, braze-ons (water bottle and rack/fender fittings, derailleur cable guides, brake cable tunnels, pump and chain hanger pegs), *et cetera*. Bikes in this range most often have an obvious better look to their frames and paint jobs, and a higher-quality finish to components, than that found in lower-priced bikes. If you plan to use your bike hard, buy carefully in this category.

After a few days of comparison shopping, trust your eye to give you hints about the value of component groups. You will find yourself quickly drawn to better equipment. Do not hesitate to ask salesmen and, especially, shop mechanics for their frank opinions of competitors' bikes. In most shops you will be dealing with fellow riders whose strong opinions are formed more by trail miles than industry hype.

A few particulars to look for (or at least think about) when considering bikes in this price range:

1. *frame*—look for well-finished, lightweight Japanese (or other good-quality) frames when deciding to invest this much money in a mountain bike, and test ride with frame flex and quickness in mind. There are some aluminum bikes offered now in this price range; compare their ride with the more common chro-moly (or "cro-mo," both shortened versions of chrome-molybdenum) frames. You will probably find them somewhat stiffer, and a bit lighter.

Double eyelet braze-ons
over rear axle.

Water bottle mount braze-ons.

2. *braze-ons*—especially at the upper end of this range you should expect these convenient additions, including multiple (most commonly two) water-bottle fittings.

3. *seat-tube reinforcement*—check for a beefed-up seat tube where the quick-release lever fits. As many riders choose bikes in this range for hard trail use, and because riders often lower saddles on steep descents and raise them again to allow leg extension on climbs, a reinforced seat tube is necessary to handle the abuse without metal fatigue.

Reinforced seat tube.

4. *seatpost length*—the longer the seatpost the greater your safe adjustment potential.

5. *wheels*—look for the strength of an aluminum-alloy rim like the RM 20, or something comparable. Tires should absolutely be skinwall (not gum), and spokes stainless steel. Sealed bearings.

6. *components*—should be of lightweight, strong alloy (not steel or plastic in the upper part of this price range), with a crisp, sharp feel to the gears and brakes. I prefer independently mounted gear shift levers and brake handles; on less-expensive bikes it is common to find these attached—allowing no independent repositioning on the handlebar for a personal fit. Look too for a sealed headset, good stem (again, this can be determined by comparison with lesser bikes and discussions with salesmen and mechanics at several shops), and bars that fit your particular riding style. Most often commuters will want swept-back bars which allow an upright, watch-the-traffic saddle position; trail riders choose "flatter" bars (straighter across) which they can lean over and still control.

At the upper end of this price range you can also expect cro-moly pedals, hub axles and brake arms (in place of steel). These are the kinds of expensive improvements over the lower category which add up to a weight savings and more lively ride. (Brake pads should also be very wide. Undersized pads are sometimes found on less-expensive bikes.)

7. *gear spread*—I'll be saying a lot about this subject momentarily, but for now I will only caution that no matter how much you drop on a bike it won't feel good on stiff climbs if you're undergeared. Likewise, it will rob you of the nearly effortless speed that comes our way when tailwinds blow and we're on hard surfaces. Especially in this price category a bike shop should consider setting you up with a wide-ranging cluster and crankset, at a slight additional charge, of course.

You will probably find the stock gears of a 28/38/48 crankset, and a free-wheel cluster of 14–30. The resulting gear inch range (this term, and its derivation, are explained later) on a 26″ wheel gear chart is 24 to 89—insufficient even for optimal touring conditions. My preference is a crankset of 24/38/48, and a cluster of 13–34, obtainable with most derailleur/dropout combinations. ("Dropouts" are the frame indentations which accept the wheel axles.) The resulting wide gear range of my preferred setup is 18 to 96—excellent both for tough trail climbs and most pavement commuting. My single reservation would come if I planned to use the extremely high-pressure slicks (treadless tires) for speed about town, and had to cover long distances on my daily commute. In that case I would drop my 13-tooth cog on my freewheel to a 12, thereby gaining a very speedy 104-inch gear.

Independently mounted gear shift lever and brake handle.

One-piece gear shift lever and brake handle.

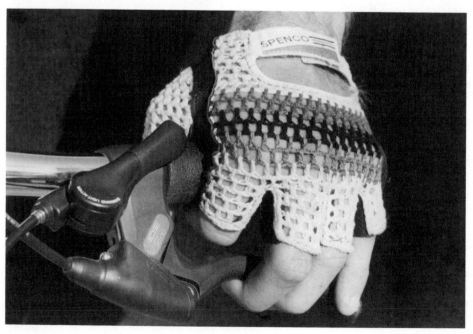

Flat, bull-moose style stem.

Single-piece ATB stem; flat handlebars.

$700 up

This is the category of the sophisticate, the rider who demands (and can afford) the best, the mountain biker who expects to challenge both his mount and himself on the toughest terrains.

More than anything, however, this is the realm of two-wheeled beauty. Framesets feel light and airy in the hand, eager to eat up the miles. Components (some of the best money can buy) gleam, work beautifully, live long and useful lives. And, if you want to drop even more money, you can have a bike custom made to fit you like a suit. Or invest between a grand and $2500 in the more exotic non-custom carbon fiber, composite, and titanium frames.

Are $700 bikes worth the money? Part of the answer will come after much comparison shopping. A better answer comes when you ride them hard. For those that cost twice that amount, the price ratchets upward far faster than a corresponding increase in performance. But then, beauty has its price.

BIKE FIT

It is unfortunately true that most people think only in terms of height when it comes to bike fit. They may purchase a bike that fits their legs, but not always their upper torso. While few bike shops these days will fail to match the entire human to the machine, it's still a good idea to know what to look for yourself.

Height —When straddling a bike I like an inch of clearance over the top on thin tires, and between two and four inches clearance on ATBs—depending on what kind of riding I intend to do. I therefore arrive at the shop in the shoes I plan to pedal in, and with my mind made up (if it's a mountain bike I'm after) about how I will ride most often—commuting, cross-over (road and trail) touring, or primarily trail.

Many of my friends are hard-core trail addicts, and as such choose bikes which provide between three and four full inches of clearance. These smaller frames offer far more maneuverability, as well as a greater chance to bail out of a fall without making memorable contact with a rock-hard top tube.

Those who use mountain bikes primarily around town, on tour, on hard-packed dirt roads and relatively easy trails, will probably find two or three inches of clearance to be sufficient. (I fall into this category, as the amusement-park approach to riding—the thrills of steep descents and challenge of "hairy" trails—is not my first love. Besides, I almost never ride the backcountry without my cameras, and they serve as a wonderfully convenient excuse to walk my bike down the worst descents.) Larger frames allow more room for water bottles on tour, generally longer chainstays which make for unencumbered pedaling when panniers are mounted, and more of the desirable thin-tire touring-bike feel (when being used for pavement thin-tire purposes) while retaining dirt-road and trail capabilities.

Length —this is where many cyclists foul up when choosing bikes. Buy a rig with too long a top tube for your combined arm and upper torso length and you'll be uncomfortably stretched when reaching for the handlebars. Buy a bike that's too short and you'll find yourself hanging over the handlebars, in too forward a position while pedaling to gain much leverage when trying to lift the front tire.

So what's the proper length? It's what you find comfortable—within the realm of what will work for your riding style. For example, as already stated commuters usually prefer a more upright saddle position than trail riders, as they can watch traffic more easily when sitting up. However, a straight-backed, George-Washington-in-the-saddle pose will rob you of much power. How? First, because you lose the increased strength gained by crouching forward (think of how we tuck our legs beneath ourselves and lean forward when rising from a chair or leaping forward). Second, because in an upright position we cannot use our arm and shoulder strength to pull the bars toward us, easing the strain of pedaling.

If you don't already know what saddle position you prefer, test ride a few bikes with varying top tube lengths and handlebar shapes. I find a comfortable fit with bars swept back slightly, and a top tube length that keeps my back at roughly a forty-five-degree angle (except of course when really leaning over the bars for steep trail ascents). A few shops determine correct fit in a similar manner to that of thin-tire bikes. They have their buyers sit in the saddle, lean to the bars, and watch to see that the middle of the knee is directly over the pedal when the foot is held at three o'clock. Others have been known to drop a plumb line from the rider's nose, making sure it lands a half inch or so behind the handlebars.

But most are not this technical, choosing instead to match the bike and biker through the use of a trained eye, to question the prospective buyer about comfort during test rides, and to make slight fore/aft saddle adjustments and changes in bar and saddle height to fine-tune the fit. (Saddles can be moved some two inches or so along the rails, thereby changing one's reach to the bars. But know that when moving the saddle forward you are also moving your center of gravity—the midpoint of your body weight—away from the rear wheel, and thereby reducing traction.)

Handlebar width —you will find great differences in bar widths, and should test ride several to find the size most comfortable for you. My preferences, as well as that of many of my riding partners, is a bar roughly equal to my shoulder width.

And now a word of solace for those of you who already own bikes that do not fit perfectly, or are considering the purchase of used bikes that *almost* fit. Short of changing the frame, consider the following alterations:

1. *handlebar/stem*—most ATB's have multi-piece bars and stem, allowing inexpensive changes to facilitate size and riding style variations. Let's say your present bike's top tube is a bit too long for your arms. First take a look at your stem; if it is a medium-to-long stem it can be replaced with a shorter one. Next, try adding bars that sweep back a bit more toward the saddle. If, on the other hand, you find yourself with too short a top tube and are hanging over the bars, purchase a high-rise stem with the greatest possible forward length extension. And if the bars are swept back at all, try a flatter style. If the bike is too short overall (in height), try a stem that is longer both vertically and in 'rise'.

2. *saddle fore/aft*—as mentioned above, the saddle can be moved a couple inches along its rails to increase or decrease distance to the handlebars.

3. *seatpost*—some very long, very strong posts are now available for those with shorter frames. Realize, however, that compensating for a too-short frame by greatly extending the saddle both raises your center of gravity (decreasing stability) and transfers it back toward the rear tire. (Greater traction results when one's weight is over the rear wheel, but a harsher ride is also noticeable.)

4. *handgrips/width/ girth*—bar width can be trimmed with a hacksaw, and also increased slightly through the addition of longer foam grips. These grips cannot, of course, extend much past the bar. However, to make a Cannondale fit perfectly two years ago I needed only that extra half inch on either side that a pair of grips (flared somewhat at the ends) provided.

I have rather large hands, and so prefer the thickest, most dense foam available to avoid foam breakdown on long backcountry tours. Consider the Grab On MTN-1 ATB grips if you want these qualities and a flared tip.

5. *crankarm length*—some long-legged riders prefer crankarms of greater than standard length (usually a change from the stock 170mm to 175mm), feeling their pedal power is increased when attempting to "torque" up steep grades. As with almost all aspects of cycling (and life), however, there is a trade off. Longer cranks can be trouble when attempting to pedal while in tight leans and curves, and also will strike more obstacles along the trail.

6. *wheel size*—a rather drastic and expensive measure to reduce bike height, the standard 26″ diameter wheels can be replaced with 24″.

FRAME COMPOSITION, CONSTRUCTION, GEOMETRY

The literature on this subject is exhaustive, and more surges our way each spring with the new onslaughts of bikes, bike magazines, and books on ATBs. Why this proliferation? That's easy: manufacturer marketing departments need to sell bikes, and writers need to sell words. And thus relatively minute differences in metallurgy, bonding techniques, tube angles and chainstay lengths are blown all out of proportion.

I'm not saying these things aren't of critical importance to racers. But the rest of us, all but the extremely hard-core, live-for-the-saddle cyclists who spend a lot of time comparing bikes, would be hard put to identify an aluminum vs. chro-moly ride while blindfolded. Besides, the same bikes perform differently for different riders because we, like the bikes, aren't all made the same.

I am therefore going to provide a general overview of this subject, address the extremes in terms of frame angles, and then suggest that you make your final decision based upon the approach described above: visit the bike shops, listen to the salesmen, read the latest magazine articles if you're particularly interested in recent technical offerings, and then test ride a bunch of bikes.

Frame Composition

The frame tubes of most mountain bikes are made of either chrome-molybdenum or aluminum. Chro-moly is lighter and stronger than other steels; aluminum is one-third the weight of steel, but only one-third as rigid, and therefore must be used in larger or thicker tubing or in other ways made strong enough to withstand years of trail bashing. Large aluminum tubing is fine in the "main triangle" (formed by the top, down and seat tubes), but causes space problems in the "rear triangle" (produced by the seat tube, seatstays and chainstays) when large off-road tires are desired. For this reason some bikes are available with aluminum main tubes and chro-moly stays; the steel alloy stays provide sufficient strength and rigidity in small-tubing size to leave plenty of room for the largest of tires.

There are many exotic metals which are being tested and offered for ATB frames, like titanium (the same stuff that makes up so much of the F–16) and the composites of carbon fiber and fiberglass, but these are still quite expensive and therefore exist somewhat beyond the realm of this introductory book on ATBs. Far more common offerings in the bike shops are the lower-priced frames which offer a chro-moly main triangle, and a high-tensile steel fork, chainstays, and seatstays. Some bikes have a chro-moly main triangle and fork (a good idea, given the tremendous amount of pressure applied to forks on rough trails), and high-tensile steel only in the "stays" (more shop shorthand, referring to the seatstays and chainstays).

A fourth type of tubing is manganese-steel, stronger and lighter than high-tensile, and more expensive. Don't get confused! Simply remember that chro-moly steel alloy is the best steel around for lightness and strength, then manganese- and high-tensile steel, in descending order.

Back to aluminum for a moment, to deal with the usual questions of how strong and "stiff" (a no-lateral-sway feeling while in the saddle) a metal this is compared to chro-moly. It all depends upon the articles you read, the test results you peruse, the kinds of frames sold in whichever bike shop you visit. Wade into the morass of "facts" on this issue and a current general opinion floats to the top: aluminum frames are *almost* as strong as, and certainly stiffer than, chro-moly. But they won't last as long and can't be bent back into shape after a crash.

I use the water metaphor for a reason, for the image of an opinion bobbing boat-like in the ocean will help keep the thought in mind that such opinions move up and down in popularity according to whichever recent article or study is getting the most play. More succinctly, the answer to the which-is-stronger question is still a pair of sixes. Personally, after many years of thrashing both chro-moly and aluminum frames, during month-long winter tours while packing extremely heavy loads and *never* experiencing a single "metal fatigue" problem, the issue for me is moot. If you're a metallurgist, you'll have a field day making your choice. The rest of us will probably end up choosing the frame that feels the best.

On the second point (stiffness), for a long time I didn't consider myself a sufficiently discriminating rider to judge frames: some aluminum frames felt less stiff to me than chro-moly, others more so. Surely, I thought, I was failing in my perceptions. After all, the heavy weight of accepted general opinion held a view quite different from mine.

But then there began to surface articles that supported my shoulder-shrug who-knows? view on the issue. And other bikers whose opinions I trust explained their personal findings: any frame material can be *made* soft or stiff; the metal, frame geometry, chainstay length, construction technique, and so on, are the determining factors. Which means that once again we're back to the importance of test riding many bikes.

A quick additional word on this topic: Many people fall into "the-stiffer-the-better" school, without thinking of the effect that such a harsh-riding bike can have on the all-day recreational cyclist. A certain degree of flexibility reduces a rider's forward progress very little in the trade off for greatly increased comfort in the saddle. Exactly how much flex you'll want in your frame can only be determined by you.

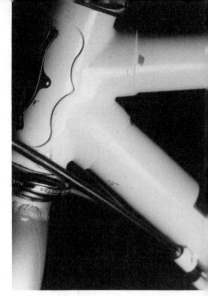

TIG welded frame.   Fillet-brazed frame.   Lugged frame.

Frame Construction

A quick tour of almost any good bike shop will provide examples of the two most common construction methods: TIG welding (the use of tungsten inert gas to weld together tubes without employing lugs), and brass brazing with lugs. (A "lug" is a metal sleeve that accepts, surrounds, and joins two tubes. See photo.) A third method of combining tubes is fillet brazing (no lugs), which you will find in specialty shops on high-end, handmade frames.

Notice that in the photographs a TIG weld is open to view; sloppy work with pinholes and gaps can be seen by the discriminating buyer. Fillet brazing (where brass is built up over the tube joint) and lugged frames, on the other hand, hide the actual tube contact point. These facts should lead the careful buyer to inspect TIG welds, and to trust only those manufacturers and specialty frame builders with a good reputation (and/or a good frame guarantee) when lugged and fillet-brazed bikes are considered.

You will find present on many frames various decals trumpeting "butted" tubes. This refers to the hollow tube's wall thickness. In a non-butted frame the walls are the same thickness throughout. A butted tube, however, has thinner walls near the tube center (where stress is lowest), and thicker walls at either end (where strength is most needed)—just as in a human's arms and legs. The result is strength *and* light weight.

Other possibly confusing frame decal terms you'll encounter are those offered by Miyata—frames which are "triple butted" and "splined." In this case the tubing is of three different thicknesses (depending upon stress requirements), and rifled (like a gun barrel) to deter the torsion stress that occurs through the twisting, side-to-side action of pedaling. (The same company offers an aluminum alloy that can be welded, rather than "bonded" like most aluminum frames. You will also notice that companies offer aluminum tubing of different diameters. Larger tubes are used when the aluminum tube wall is to be thin; thinner tubing has thicker walls. I've ridden both extensively and honestly cannot tell the difference.)

Frame Geometry

If you think the material above is confusing, wait until you enter the world of angles and other frame measurements. Look at the drawing and you'll see what forms the head tube angle, bottom bracket height, chainstay length, and so forth. That's the easy part. The trick is understanding how these numbers affect a ride.

It is perhaps best to talk first about bikes at either extreme. Racing ATBs have "steep" angles, while mountain bikes designed for beach cruising are said to possess "relaxed" geometry. But before these terms can make any sense you must be able to visualize what the words imply; only the engineers among us can "see" the difference between, say, a 69 and 72-degree angle. (I hesitate to give definite numbers, as I feel they mean so little unless considered along with all the other bike and biker factors involved. But many cyclists today who want bikes for paved, dirt-road and trail use combined choose frames with head tubes in the 69-70 degree range.)

Take another look at the frame geometry drawing. Notice "C"—the head-tube angle measurement. Think of the head tube lying flat upon the frame's top tube; this would of course be an angle of 0 degrees. As the head tube rises (stands up) it increases in angle, or grows steeper. At one point it will reach 69 degrees, and if it continues moving vertically three degrees more it will be at our 72 degree angle mentioned above.

For an easier image think of relaxed, laid-back angles as a person reclining in an easy chair, and steeper angles as that same person in a straight-backed office chair while writing at a desk. Board a laid-back beach cruiser bike and you'll feel the easy steering and cushy ride. That's great for the dunes, but unworkable for tough climbs up mountain grades when you need instead to be leaning forward into the task. On the other hand, the at-work, canted-forward position of racing bikes is perfect for rough climbs. But they're lousy for a beach.

Use these same images while working your way through the seat tube angle concept. More a function of leg length, overall height, and a matter of positioning the body relative to the crankarms (to put the knee, roughly, over the pedal when it is at three o'clock), a "standard" seat tube angle for all-purpose use is even harder to suggest than head tubes.

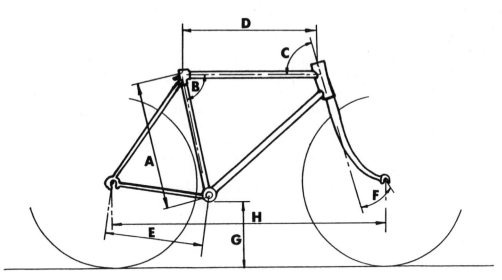

Frame geometry.
A) *seat-tube length*   E) *chainstay length*
B) *seat-tube angle*   F) *fork rake*
C) *head-tube angle*   G) *bottom bracket height*
D) *top-tube length*   H) *wheel base*

Fork rake is most easily seen when racing and touring ATBs are set next to one another. The racing fork will be almost straight, transmitting the feel of every front-wheel bump directly to the rider's hands. This (and a steep head tube) allows the expert rider an opportunity for extremely precise steering, but a longer fork rake makes this steering much easier (especially on descents). And that is what's desirable to most mountain bikers.

Now to bottom bracket height, wheel base, and chainstay length. An ATB's bottom bracket (most are in the 11″ to 12″ range) is higher than a similar-size touring bike, to allow for ground clearance over obstacles and the ability to pedal without striking objects on the trail and in tight turns. Mountain bikes generally have a somewhat longer wheelbase than touring bikes, for bet-

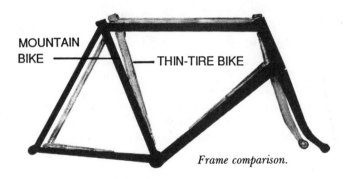

MOUNTAIN
BIKE ——————— THIN-TIRE BIKE

Frame comparison.

ter shock absorption and greater steering ability (through shallower angles) off road. Now look at the drawing again and imagine extremely long chainstays. Do you see that as these stays increase in length the rear tire is pushed away from the saddle? The importance here is that as chainstays are lengthened the body's weight (located primarily in the saddle) is less and less over the rear tire, therefore lessening traction. A bike with a long wheelbase and long chainstays is far more gentle to ride, but not as good (or as "quick") around turns and far more difficult on tough off-road climbs.

There has been of late an almost across-the-board movement toward shorter chainstays, to bring the rear wheel back up beneath the saddle and so provide the rider with greater traction and quickness in handling. Racing bikes have very short chainstays (and extremely harsh rides); touring ATBs have much longer chainstays. Most cross-duty bikes will probably have them in the 17" to 17½" range. If you have large feet and are considering somewhat short chainstays you might position a rack over the rear tire, have the salesman hold a pannier in place, and see if your heel will strike the bag on the upstroke.

GEARING

I said earlier that you will probably find the following stock gears on the mountain bikes you test ride: chainrings of 28/38/48; a freewheel of 14–30 (for a gear inch range of 24 to 89). I added that in my opinion such a bike is woefully undergeared in both extremes—not "low" enough (easy to pedal) for very steep off-road climbs, and not "high" enough (hard to pedal) for riding pavement with high-pressure tires. My preference is a crankset of 24/38/48, and a cluster of 13–34 (for a very wide gear range of 18 to 96). And, if I planned to use the very high-pressure slicks (treadless tires) for speed about town, and had to cover long distances on my daily commute, I would drop the 13-tooth freewheel cog to a 12—thereby producing a huge 104-inch gear.

It is my expectation that the industry will in time move in this wide-gear-range direction, as most component groupings now found on the bikes can handle the spread. (Some components and dropout configurations will keep you from dropping the smallest chainring further than a 26, or increasing the largest freewheel cog beyond a 32. Your bike shop will be able to guide you in this.) Until then, you must decide if your intended cycling will justify the increased cost involved in making these changes.

An inventor in Albuquerque has developed a novel way to retain the standard triple chainring (and therefore the quick, easy shifting inherent in a relatively tight gear pattern) and still acquire lower gears. In fact, a rider who anticipates extremely heavy loads, or the toughest hills, or who wishes to climb trees with his bike, now has the option of adding a Mountain Tamer Quad—a *fourth* chainring. The Quad comes in sizes of 21 to 16 teeth, for an incredibly low gear inch of 12 when used with a 34-tooth freewheel cog! (Address in Appendix.)

And now it's time to learn the derivation of "gear inch." I'll borrow my two-page discussion of this issue from my book on cycle touring, *Touring on Two Wheels:*

Many (thin-tire) bike manufacturers publish literature on their cycles stating something like "33 to 101 gear range as equipped," or "100-inch gear high range." What is a 100-inch gear, and how is that number derived? It comes from this formula:

$$\frac{\# \text{ teeth in front sprocket}}{\# \text{ teeth in rear sprocket}} \times \text{wheel diameter in inches}$$

Take my touring bike, for example: the larger front sprocket has 54 teeth, the smallest back sprocket has 14.

$$\frac{54}{14} \times 27 = 104 \text{ inch gear}$$

But this does *not* mean the bike will travel 104 inches down the road with one pump of the pedals. It refers instead to the number of inches in diameter the front wheel would be in a "direct-drive" setup, such as the old "high-wheelers" of the 1870s and 1880s. Those bikes had no complicated gearing, and therefore the single "gear" was determined by the size of the front wheel, to which the pedals were attached. Imagine a high-wheeler 104 inches in diameter, or more than 8½ feet high!

On the other end of the scale the lowest gear on my bike is 33.3 inches:

$$\frac{42}{34} \times 27 = 33.3$$

In this case the "high-wheeler" wouldn't be so high at all, and would look more like a child's tricycle. Now you can see the beauty of today's gearing, which provides for such extremes of great speed and hill-climbing potential, and all the ratios between.

I know it's confusing. But you can make things far easier by looking closely at a bike. Imagine the chain affixed to the largest chainring, and the smallest freewheel cog (thus the "highest"—hardest—gear). Let's assume the chainring is three times the size of the rear cog. In this case, each time the pedals revolve once (that is, each the chainring is turned one time) the rear wheel will spin around three times. How far will that propel you down the road? That's easy, even without resorting to higher mathematics. Using a standard [thin-tire] 27″ diameter wheel, we merely multiply this diameter by pi to obtain the circumference, then multiply again by three revolutions.

$$27″ \times 3.14 = 84.78″ \text{ (or about 7 feet for one revolution)}$$

$$7′ \times 3 \text{ revolutions} = 21 \text{ feet}$$

Now, imagine the chain on the smallest chainring and the largest cog in the rear. Many triple cranksets have sprockets as small as and even smaller than the largest freewheel cog, but for our discussion we will imagine they are identical in size (possessing the same number of teeth). In this case (a one-to-one gear ratio), each time the rider pedals once the rear wheel revolves only once. And from the figures above we already know the bike would proceed only seven feet forward.

It stands to reason that moving seven feet with each pedal revolution would be far easier than propeling oneself twenty-one feet. When going uphill, therefore, and interested more in being able to continue pedaling than in covering distances quickly, we switch into our lower (easier) gears. When the

Gear ratios.

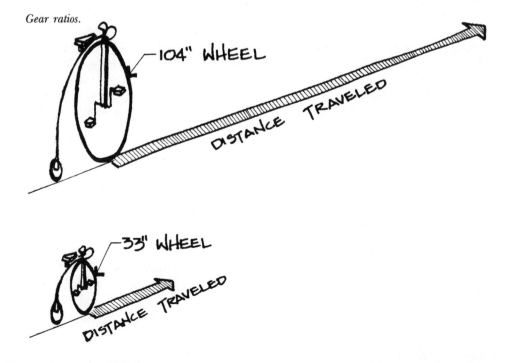

summit is attained, or on the flat with the wind at our backs, the relative ease of pedaling and our gear options allow us to take advantage of the situation by switching into high (harder) gears. Think of hiking up a hill, when you take short steps, compared to your long, easy strides on level ground. The principle is the same.

We're almost finished with gearing. Simply reduce all the numbers provided above for a mountain bike (a much more stable 26″ diameter wheel instead of the thin-tire 27″ standard), and watch your chain placement until you get the hang of how each gear feels. You'll soon find that the numbers are important guides when buying a bike or setting up a new chainring/freewheel configuration for a specific purpose, but that few riders ever pay attention to their gear inches while in the saddle.

I've received criticism over the years for my gear range suggestions. People have written to say my setup reproduces gears: that is, I fail to obtain eighteen different gears on an eighteen-speed bike. It's true—but to me it doesn't matter. It would if I were racing, but in both my thin-tire and ATB commuting/touring/fun riding I am far more interested in well-spaced jumps between my chainrings and freewheel sprockets, and especially the ultimate extremes. (My preferred spread in mountain bike freewheels is 13-16-19-23-28-34.)

For those of you who will rush off to buy a bike before reading any of the remaining chapters, the following are additional items for consideration.

> *brake lever "reach"*—riders with small hands should take care to purchase brake levers in which the reach between handlebar and the large, motorcycle-type lever is not difficult to span. If the reach is too great your reaction time will be increased when needing to apply the brakes (a possibly dangerous situation on trail or in traffic), and the muscle strain of long descents will be sorely greater. Many bikes now come with "adjustable-reach" levers.
>
> *rack/fender eyelets*—commuters, and some tourers, will definitely want *both* rack and fender braze-on eyelets front and rear. These allow for a much easier and secure attachment to the bike. (If you find yourself with single eyelets only you might consider investing in the excellent Bruce Gordon racks, which have separate fender attachment points on the support arms.)
>
> *clips/straps*—trail riding requires them, and your touring and commuting will also be much more efficient with their use.

2

Accessories

IF YOU THOUGHT you could put away your wallet after deciding upon and buying a bike, think again. Sure you've got the mount itself, a sleek beast capable of carrying you into (and *out* of) the wilds of city and trail. But what if it rains? Or you get a flat? And what if you want to pack a lunch and first-aid kit into the backcountry, or your books to school or briefcase to the office? Which shoes are best for off-road travel? Should you wear a helmet? What's the best way to lock a bike, especially one with a quick-release wheel and seatpost?

Come on, smile. Sure it means making more decisions, and it can mean spending more if you don't go about it carefully. But this chapter is designed first to let you know the kinds of products available to make your time in the saddle more pleasant, and second, to help you keep more money in your pocket, and your bike out of someone else's garage.

My primary purpose is to inform you of the existence of the kinds of products available and the need for them, *not* to suggest one brand name over another. Also please recall my words in the Introduction about the impossibility of a book being encyclopedic on mountain biking, due to publication lag time and the fast-developing sport of ATBs. With this in mind, use the following guidance toward products to direct you to and help you assess both the older and most recent offerings in the mountain bike world.

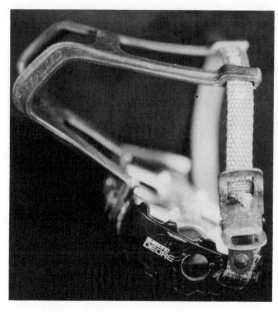

"Mountainclip."

Bike

I've mentioned a few of these accessory items in Chapter One, but they bear repeating here as reminders for use in town and on trail.

Clips/Straps/Pedal Reflectors At first glance the use of clips and straps on an ATB might appear suicidal. "What? Be locked to a bike that's bouncing over curbs and boulders?!" The concern is understandable, but you will learn very quickly that no matter what the terrain, your control (and therefore your safety) is greatly increased when your feet will not slip from the pedals. Newcomers will please notice that I did not say *locked* to the pedals. Straps *can* be pulled tight, but are not by most thin- and fat-tire riders alike. And, in the event that gravity wins out over your bike-handling abilities, your feet will slip free almost automatically.

In the field of "regular" clip/strap combinations Specialized offers a "Mountainclip" with an extremely wide mouth, a good idea given the far beefier shoes worn by fat-tire cyclists compared to tourers. These clips also have a raised toe area, designed to fit the higher "toe box" of ATB boots and shoes.

Concerning the pedals themselves, the more expensive models are made of strong, weight-saving alloy rather than steel. The "rat-trap" edges must be pronounced to allow a firm grip while bouncing about, and you will notice the results on your shins until you learn to be careful about pedal placement. Plastic composite pedals do exist, but though their edges are therefore far kinder to the shins they do not, for me, afford a sufficient grip.

Rough-and-tumble trail riders often view my pedal reflectors with disdain. And I'll grant that I've never had the need for them while single-tracking through the mountains. But very often I find myself returning to a trail head at dark, necessitating a short pavement ride back home or to a car. The pedal reflectors, so crucial always when commuting (due to their great visibility resulting from the near-constant up and down movement), give an edge of safety on dark country or canyon roads.

Mirror I have yet to find a single, completely satisfactory ATB mirror. The models which insert into the hollow handlebar tube end are, for me, forever working their way free (a result I think of the bike lying at times on its left side). Mirrors that employ a molded plastic sleeve to cup the handlebar grip, held in place by a large cordura strap, are too bulky even for my large hands. The result is either an insecure hold on one's left grip (very problematic on trails, where every nuance must be felt and reacted to, and even a discomfort when commuting and especially on tours), or a movement of the left hand closer to the stem.

I make it a habit to remove my cordura-strapped mirror for trails, and though this and the reattaachment time add up to only a few minutes it is time I would prefer not to lose. Helmet and eyeglass wearers have several choices of mirrors the size of those used in dentist offices.

Water Bottle Cages/Water Bottles I was among the first to scoff at "mountain cages," those bottle holders trumpeted to withstand the abuse of tough trails. Industry hype, I figured. But after several years of seeing what happens to regular thin-tire cages when stressed in ways for which they were not designed (i.e., trail bashing), especially when holding the large-capacity water bottles, I bow my head to the engineers.

Drop a few more dollars and you can buy both strength and extreme light weight in the dauntingly named "injection-molded carbon fiber composites."

All water bottles themselves are not created equal. Buy the cheap ones and they'll crush when you push the lid down tight. Better bottles are formed of denser plastic walls, to withstand a gloved and haphazard hand smashing the lid upon the bottle lip. And they won't leak when tipped on their sides.

Larger bottles hold twenty-eight ounces (just four shy of a quart); the smaller hold twenty. How many do you need? A human working hard in ninety-degree heat needs ten quarts (that's two-and-a-half *gallons*) of water replenishment every day. And while riding trails is tremendous fun, your body still interprets it as hard work. There's also the problem of one's body actually becoming slightly dehydrated before the mouth feels thirsty, bringing on an old bikers' maxim: Eat before you're hungry, drink before you're thirsty.

I pack along two full large waterbottles for most day trail rides, though I have mounted as many as eight (yes, eight) for extended desert trips. (And, of course, packed along a water purifier and a host of prayers that I'd find springs or sandstone pools of snowmelt.) Water weighs eight pounds per gallon, so you'll want to go as light as possible. But keep replenishment in mind.

If I were ordering a handmade frame I would have four water bottle cage braze-ons added, for my long tours with heavy loads. Three (and a purifier) will get me through even the hottest shorter trails. Two cage braze-ons is what you'll find on most production bikes, so invest in a leak-proof bottle or two for your panniers.

Handlebar Grips I discussed the fact in Chapter 1 that replacement bar grips are available in various degrees of density, girth, and length. Those with longish, flared ends extend the bar width very slightly, but noticeably.

Tires First, buy skinwalls—not the heavy, dead-feeling gum rubber. Second, it makes sense that wide, low-pressure, full-knobby tires provide the best traction in dirt, and the poorest on-pavement performance. Third, those people who use their ATBs for urban commutes exclusively will want high-pressure, fast-rolling skins which spin on unbroken beads of rubber.

As you would expect, manufacturers have observed these needs and rushed to fill them. Tires exist for every specialty (the Specialized Hardpack off-roader, 26 × 2.2, 35–80 psi, for instance, and the same company's extremely lightweight, thin, no-tread commuting beauty called the Fat Boy, 26 × 1.25, 100 psi). And for those of us who ride often on all terrains, and do not like changing tires and can't afford a separate set of wheels, there are variable-pressure, interlocking knob tires like the Specialized Crossroads II and Ritchey Quad. Somewhat thinner than the full off-roaders (1.95″ and 1.9″, respectively), these can be dropped in pressure for increased traction when in dirt and pumped up hard for pavement.

Specialized Hardpack tire.   *Tioga Farmer John tire.*   *Crossroads II tire.*

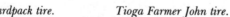

Mountain bike flats are very few and far between compared to thin-tires, but that's little consolation when you arrive late at class, the factory or office because of debris-strewn city streets. Keep your boss happy by installing "tire liners" (Mr. Tuffy is one popular brand), thin plastic sheaths which line the tire and therefore protect the fragile tube from intruders. These are also a great idea for riders who travel in cactus country.

Bike Security (Seat Leash, Hite-Rite, U-Locks) I spoke earlier of theft problems when it comes to quick-release seatposts. These are an excellent idea for trail riding, which requires either the raising and lowering of the saddle for steep hill climbs and descents, or the learning of a far more skilled rear-end-off-the-saddle technique on downhills. But this mechanism is also appreciated by the world's kleptos: in an instant you can lose an expensive seatpost and saddle.

The quick-release seatpost bolt can be replaced by a two-inch long, six-millimeter bolt, double nutted on one end for security. That will take care of casual theft, but you won't be able to alter your saddle's height at the flip of a lever. Two products now provide theft protection while retaining the quick-release ability. The Seat Leash is a black, PVC-coated ³⁄₃₂″ galvanized aircraft cable that loops around the saddle rails on one end, and the seatstay at the other. Granted, a small pair of wire cutters can quickly make it history. But then it's often too conspicuous for a criminal to have at a seatpost with a tool.

Seat leash.   *Hite-Rite.*

The Hite-Rite provides protection and another service as well (one you'll learn more about in the next chapter)—that of allowing in-the-saddle height adjustments. Just reach down while coasting along and trip the lever, push down with your rear end or let the strong metal spring push the saddle up toward you, and close the lever again. Presto. Another important point: the saddle always remains "centered" with the Hite-Rite (the nose remains perfectly in line with the top tube).

Then there's the chore of hanging on to one's quick-release front wheel, and the entire bike. Most riders have gravitated away from heavy cables to the greater security provided by U-locks, still rather weighty at almost two pounds. I've been using Citadels for years; Kryptonite is but one more well-known name in these protectors. These can be carried easily inside a bike bag, in the space designed for them beneath some "rack trunks" (bags designed to ride on the top of the rear luggage rack), and, with some saddles, hanging from the rails. Rhode Gear, a particularly innovative company when it comes to accessories, offers a "Snap-Lok Bracket" that mounts either to one's water-bottle braze-ons or with non-marring clips around a frame tube, to provide quick-release access and storage of a lock. Extra-long U-locks, handy when locking to something other than a bike rack and also to secure both front wheel and frame at the same time, are also available. (Some U-locks carry bike-theft warranties up to $1000.)

Though U-locks provide the greatest security available, there are two current techniques (thankfully obvious and rather noisy) for busting them apart. I take my bike with me when I can, and park it in very public places when it's left unguarded.

Shark Fin Named for its distinctive shape, this thin piece of plastic adheres to the right-side chainstay to protect the paint from "chainslap" (the scratching that can result from a bouncing chain on trail rides), and to guard against "chaingrab" (when a loose chain falls between the stay and inside

Citadel U-lock in Rhode Gear Snap-Lok bracket.

Shark Fin.

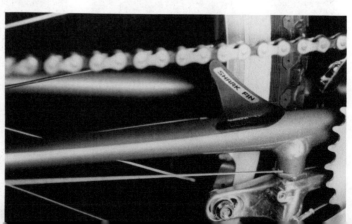

chainring). Most riders attempt to keep their chains in chainring/freewheel cog combinations which make the chain too taut to fly about, but no one's perfect.

Air Pump Hand pumping has never been among my favorite pastimes, and filling a huge ATB tire (even with less air pressure, usually, than thinner tires) makes the act even less desirable. But it still beats walking. Larger-volume pumps now exist to cut down the time you'll spend flailing away, and some are sufficiently short to fit inside bike bags. (Be *sure* your pump is securely mounted if you're affixing it to the frame and are heading for the trails.) And if you're really lazy and/or in a hurry, there's a compressed-gas cartridge/brass inflator kit available. But you'll pay a hefty price for the convenience.

Fenders I'll have more to say on these in the chapter on commuting, but for now you should know they are available in various lengths and widths. And, of course, that the widest and longest "wraps" will do the best job in protecting you from the elements. You should also know that in my opinion the "rack cover" and "mini fender" (thick plastic sheets that snap onto a rear rack top and to the down tube) are worthless for keeping you clean. (Be sure to use a thread-locking compound when putting fenders on a mountain bike. In fact, I use it for all braze-on attachments.)

Racks There have been light years' of improvements in this department since my world ride in '74. Back then we used heavy racks with moveable support arms and a spring-loaded top. They connected to the seatstays with metal clamps that persisted in falling toward the center-pull brakes; they swayed in the breeze and scared us a hundred times when we thought they would crack.

A half-dozen years later, nine hundred miles into a solo winter ride along the Santa Fe Trail, another rack did break on me. But those were the old days. I test a lot of products, receive a lot of readers' letters, talk with bike magazine editors and bike shop workers on a weekly basis—and I haven't heard of *any* presently offered racks breaking on the road.

But that doesn't mean they're all the same. Starting at the top (both in quality and cost) are the Bruce Gordon racks, the chro-moly, hand-brazed, baked-on black-epoxy-finished frame extensions that look like pieces of sculpture, and ride like they were born on your bike. Next comes Blackburn, made of 6061-T6 heat-treated aluminum alloy, with specific support designs for mountain bikes. And after these industry leaders comes a host of look-alikes. Buy carefully, and when putting any rack on your bike perform the operation with care (and a little thread-locking compound). The abuse these things take from the world, and the strain under which they live, is enormous.

If you pack a lot of weight you should consider both front and rear racks. But think long and hard before you put front-wheel low-riders on your mountain bike. I've had to test these systems for a couple companies and found it

Bruce Gordon rack. *Blackburn rack.*

extremely unpleasant: fall into a deep rut and you'll end up knocking off your front panniers; try to wind through brush, cactus, or high rocks and you'll bang up your bags. Front low-riders on ATBs just don't make sense, as the shorter, wider wheels and tires of mountain bikes, and their heavy-duty frames, make them so stable that the slight amount of stability gained by the lowered center of gravity fails to offset the problems incurred.

Lights More on this in the urban jungle chapter, as it's a crucial subject for commuters. But for all of us it is good to know of a few available items.

I've already made my case for pedal reflectors. Now add a Belt Beacon, an amber taillight that attaches to your belt or rear rack and flashes once a second, and no one behind your bike has an excuse for not seeing you on the road.

So much for being seen; now comes you seeing enough of the road to make it home. Continuous-beam battery lights illuminate little of the world when fresh, and grow weak very quickly. Seatstay-mounted generators have a problem with the sideknobs of many tires; chainstay mounted generators (directly behind the bottom bracket) work well with continuous-rubber tire patterns, but cannot be affixed to bikes with U-brakes. One of the brightest alternatives is the appropriately named Brite Lite, a headlight/taillight rechargeable gell-cell battery pack system that packs a four-hour charge.

And for those who always wear a helmet and don't mind looking slightly

Front Brite Lite. *Rear Brite Lite.*

weird, there's the Cycle-Ops. The headlight attaches miner-like to the helmet front, and a coiled cable runs over the top and down your back to the battery pack. The bright halogen beam is supposed to shine for some three hours per charge. It's also a real hit at parties.

Cyclometers These aren't a necessity, but sometimes it's nice to know *exactly* how far it is to work, how quickly you've ridden a trail, how fast you're traveling during a workout. Very light and relatively easy to install, these things have grown miniscule over the past few years.

Clothing

I'll provide specific suggestions for particular riding styles in following chapters, but for now want to make a few general comments that may be of some assistance starting off.

Riding Gloves Ride hard all day on thin tires and the pressure against tiny nerves in the heels of your hands will make your two smallest fingers on each hand feel numb. Beat the trails on a mountain bike for half that long and your fingers will be both numb and sore, the latter from constant vibrations and occasional hard jolts. Regular riding gloves will do, though a few brands have a bit too much padding for my taste; especially on an ATB one must be protected from the bar, yet at the same time have a very firm grip on it. Test the various thicknesses and fabrics until you find the one that's right for you.

Let me suggest that you test the new Spenco gloves made specially for mountain bikers. The backing is vented nylon and thick terry cloth (to wipe away perspiration); the palm is a man-made "leather" that will not shrink or stiffen, and is completely washable. Spenco's well-known 'Biosoft' Gel is the internal padding, a thin layer that protects my hands sufficiently during all-day workouts but still allows complete control of the bars.

Avocet cyclometer.

Spenco gloves.

Excellent mountain bike shoe—Nike Caldera.

Excellent mountain bike boot—Nike Zealand.

Shoes Visit a well-stocked bike shop and you'll find an amazing selection of footwear designed specifically for off-road riding. My personal requirements are four: a very stiff mid-sole (to reduce pedal strain on the instep muscles); a tread that is sufficiently aggressive to allow for good traction when pushing the bike, yet not so ribbed or corrugated that it causes problems getting into and out of the clips; a wide, stiff toe box that will not compress after hours of pressure against the clips (thereby causing toe pain); and all-day comfort both in and out of the saddle.

Everyone has his or her own favorite. Mine is the somewhat heavy, all-leather-upper Nike Thunderdome (an excellent all-purpose low-cut light hiking shoe, which isn't even in Nike's extensive cycling shoe line). One of my female models, who happens to be a far more accomplished downhiller than I, prefers the extremely stiff Specialized ATB shoes. And another frequent trail rider friend likes the Hi-Tec brand, though for me these shoes have soles that are too thin and cause pain and numbness after many hours. (The soft toe box also gives me discomfort.)

But do not buy by brand alone. Designs change, new models appear and old ones fade away. And, as my personal choice indicates, do not fail to consider non-bike shoes as possibilities. (If you find one that's insufficiently stiff, but perfect in all other departments, try adding a pair of low-cost Spenco insert orthotics. Soaked in hot water they can be molded to fit your foot perfectly.)

Eyewear I wrote the following in my recent book on bike touring: "Glasses are a good idea whenever in the saddle . . . Catch a single junebug in the eyeball, or strain your eyes after days of sunny skies, and you'll know the importance of having a shield of glass or plastic between you and the world when traveling at good speed." The same is true for mountain biking, but even more so. Twigs, tree limbs, flying rock from a fellow biker's rear knobby, *any* projectile can have disastrous results.

But what to buy? Let me suggest a few guidelines based solely upon personal preferences: 1) variable-shade lenses which do not distort natural colors (these will allow you to wear your specs even in low-light conditions); 2) unbreakable lenses, so you won't be blind in case of a "header" (those unfortunate—though exhilarating if survived—spills over the handlebars); 3) preferably of a size somewhat smaller than your face, thereby not making you resemble an insect. (The third *personal* requirement is a response to an industry tendency toward the bizarre in bikers' clothing. My hope is that this extremely uncomplimentary eyewear will soon go the way of the Nehru jacket.)

No matter what you purchase, however, I strongly suggest that you make sure they will remain on your head while bouncing about (I prefer the metal earpieces which wrap fully behind the ear), and that you not get into the habit of simply laying them on your bike or handlebar bag each time you stop. My solution was to have a saddle maker design a leather belt-mounted case for my glasses; most people invest in "Chums" or a similar product—cloth strips which slip onto the earpieces and ride behind your head while being worn. When the glasses are removed they merely hang suspended from your neck.

Shorts I ride on occasion with people who prefer doing the trails in the same kind of togs worn by racers—tight-fitting lycra with chamois inserts. As with most clothing items, shorts are too personal a matter to prescribe. My personal preference is the same brand I use for my months-long tours—Sportif USA. I buy the ones that are made of an extremely durable blend of polyester/cotton/spandex (the last material allowing the shorts to stretch comfortably in all directions), with zippered back pockets, two deep front pockets, two lower-front button-down patch pockets, and a small watch pocket as well, wide belt loops, YKK zipper in front, and all stress seams double-stitched. (Notice that the "cargo" pockets unfortunately found on so many bike shorts are not present; I find these pockets will empty their contents when one is doing almost anything but pedaling.)

Helmet Buy any one which meets either the ANSI Z90.4 or Snell Memorial Foundation standards (the helmet and/or box will be labeled accordingly), and wear it. And if you know a friend or loved one who at present doesn't ensconce his skull in foam and plastic each time he boards a bike, let him know the statistics. (I recently did a pro-helmet piece specifically for children, attempting to explain the physiological reasons behind the fact that of the roughly fourteen hundred bike deaths annually, approximately seventy-five per cent result from head injuries.) If the statistics don't convince him, you might discuss the incredible advances helmet manufacturers have made in reducing weight, in increasing airflow to the scalp, and even in making the things somewhat attractive. Or work in the other direction, by explaining the far greater weight and discomfort of a coffin.

Always wear a helmet.

Tell him these facts in no uncertain terms, just as you would counsel against smoking three packs a day, ingesting lousy foods, or making a bad marriage. After all, what are friends for?

But, realize that no matter how ironclad your arguments, and even if he agrees with your reasoning, he still might choose *not* to wear a helmet, may continue to smoke, may fail to join you on the Pritikin or Fit-for-Life diet, or persist in plans to marry the carhop who's half his age. Then, no matter how much you love him, it's your turn to accept the fact that if he's an adult, and if he possesses an IQ at least in the high double digits, *the decision is ultimately his to make.* Even God grants we puny creations something called free will.

Bike Bags

I will address particular bags for commuting and touring in later chapters, and so at present will provide simply a general overview of the many different kinds of bags available.

On-person Fanny packs appear to be far more popular with mountain bikers than with thin-tire cyclists, perhaps because so many fat-tire enthusiasts prefer to keep their bikes "clean"—free of the heavy racks and packs which might impair their trail-handling abilities. If cost is a factor, consider a fanny pack or shoulder bag until you can afford the rack and other bags. If you need more room, Nike puts out a fanny pack that converts into a small backpack.

Commuters especially will be interested in two cross-the-shoulder, small-of-the-back-hugging models designed by the former New York bike messenger Paul Rosenfield. His first "Cycle Sac" is a classic beauty of heavy canvas, a rubberized waterproof inner-coating (I even trust my slides to it during a storm), a size sufficient for small art portfolios, and a design that keeps it out of the way when pedaling. Perfect for the college crowd, it also lets the rest of us remain on two wheels even when the load for the office is large.

Nike fanny pack.

Paul's Cycle Sac.

The ATB model is just a bit smaller, far lighter, constructed of waterproofed cordura, and is equipped with side-release Fastex buckles and a second strap that snaps across the torso and holds the bag against you as you beat the trails or curbs. (Address is in the Appendix.)

Rack packs/Rack duffles There are any number of rear-rack-top bags to choose from, so don't get too excited with the first model that comes into view. They differ in obvious ways—material (most often a kind of cordura), overall size, number of pockets, cost, etc., but most important is something far less noticeable to the eye: attachment. If you're thinking of this becoming your everyday commuting bag, imagine how it will be to attach and remove the bag

Cannondale rack trunk.

Robert Beckman Designs panniers.

every time you are on and off the bike.

Why not leave it in place, you say, if it's empty when you head into a store or go to work? Don't try it, for you'll lose the bag for sure. (For that matter, do not leave anything attached which can come off easily; water bottles and pumps can be gone in an instant.) There is a "duffle" available that can be left on the bike, for it is locked into place. This is the bright, waterproof, hard-shell ABS plastic "Vetta Box," with 270 cubic inches of storage and a hinged lid that secures the contents with a key.

Rhode Gear Via Cycle Satchel.

Panniers So many choices! There's only one system for me when it comes to months-long tours—Robert Beckman Designs. Built to custom fit the amazingly strong Bruce Gordon racks, I can pile in half my belongings, leave on a cross-country ride, and not give a moment's thought to rack/pack problems. (Robert Beckman Designs—formerly called Needle Works—bags are now being made to fit Blackburn-style racks as well.)

The best pannier, however, lies in the eyes of the beholder, and there are many other "good" pannier systems available. Almost any bike magazine will contain a number of pannier company advertisements; send a postcard requesting a catalogue and price sheet, visit the bike shops to see which brands they carry, and begin your search in earnest. Remember the advice given above: if you are considering a pannier as your always-present-around-town bag, pay particular attention to ease of mounting and detachment. And be sure to buy a "pannier cover" (rain cover) before you need it. The heavy cordura that most good bags are made of takes a long time to dry.

Briefcases Several companies make stylish, cordura bike briefcases which mount securely to a rack, and hide the mounting hardware (usually a spring/tension strap and hooks) nicely behind a zipper or velcro flap. Most are too much like briefcases in size to admit all the other necessities that are normally carried in a biker's "possibles bag"—poncho, tools, pump. . . . Take a look at Rhode Gear's Via Cycle Satchel and you'll see one example of a beiefcase/pannier large enough for legal briefs and other gear.

And for those who are not concerned about weight or a somewhat "klunky" look, REI (Recreational Equipment Incorporated) offers the Novara Shopping Baskets. Sized for a grocery bag and therefore a breeze for homeward bound stops at the market, they are perfect for tossing in a backpack or briefcase (if protected against the rain) and riding to work. When not in use the sides and bottoms collapse and snap closed. I suggest that if you use these you might employ a few small hose clamps to affix them permanently to the rack, thereby detering all but the most determined thief.

FIRST AID

There are a couple of ways to think about this topic; the one you choose will determine the medical-supplies portion of your "always-carry" kit. Most commuters figure since they're in a city they can count on fellow man for assistance if run down, and for the occasional minor scrape can wait until they get to work for a band-aid. Those who have ever witnessed the kind of large-area surface scrapes that can result from contact with the pavement (a wound amazingly rare even for long-time, *non*-racing bikers), however, may also trust their fellow man, but still make an effort to pack along at least those bandages necessary to stop the bleeding and protect the wound before other help arrives. In short, the division in thinking falls along the lines of those who down deep feel "not me" when it comes to accidents, and those who might think the same but prefer to be prepared.

Besides, most cross-over cyclists who sometimes spend weekends on the country roads or trails simply add a lunch to their everyday bag of bike gear, and head out. And who wants to be caught in the wilds without first-aid gear?

I suggest therefore that you glance at the following list, add to or delete from as you wish, seal the contents in double zip-lock bags, and carry it with you always.

> sunshade
> aspirin
> butterfly closure bandages (think of these as 'band-aid stitches')
> band-aids
> gauze compress pads (a half-dozen 4″ × 4″)
> gauze (1 roll)
> ace bandages or Spenco joint wraps
> Benadryl (an antihistamine to guard against allergic reactions . . . obviously for the trail, not commuting)
> water purification tablets (actually tetraglycine hydroperiodide tablets,

marketed under Portable Aqua, Coughlan's, or Globaline trade names;
I prefer filter-system water purifiers on long backcountry trips, for reasons I will state in chapter 5)
moleskin/Spenco "Second Skin"
hydrogen peroxide/iodine/Mercurochrome (some kind of antiseptic)
snakebite kit (read the directions *before* you're bitten)

It should be obvious that you will have to re-pack some of these items. I prefer using water-tight plastic 35mm film canisters (of which I have an abundance; if you don't spent a lot of time behind a lens I suggest you call a large film processing lab, as they often have empty canisters they will give away or sell for a nominal fee), which I label by writing the contents on paper, cutting out the tiny block, then taping it in place.

One last point. For cactus-country tours and even weekend desert rides, I remove my snakebite kit from the double-zip-lock kit and keep it closer to me. It is, after all, one item you will want to reach in a hurry.

Film cannisters make useful containers.

CAR RACKS

Few people wish to spend half their Saturday pedaling to trail heads and quiet country lanes, where the *real* ride begins. After a week of commuting most would rather drive to that point, which involves bike transport.

Your choice of racks will be determined by placement (where you want the bikes to sit—on the roof, behind the vehicle, standing upright in a truck bed), speed of attachment (some roof racks require removal of the bicycle's front wheel), number of bikes to be transported, and, of course, cost. Once again you will have to play the wise consumer, as finding the perfect rack for your car or truck is made difficult by the number of choices and considerations.

Wild Side Designs car rack.

Shorter riders often decide against roof racks for obvious reasons; those who worry about the slightest possible scratch on their cars usually avoid rear-window or trunk-hanging racks (though the Rhode Gear Cycle Shuttle's coated metal clamps and dense foam pads, plus a pedal "sock" covering, help to insure your vehicle against damage). Rear-mounted bikes pick up an amazing amount of dust when traveling dirt roads; roof-mounted bikes are subject to high-wind-driven moisture, as well as many of the bugs that have managed to avoid your windshield.

Removing a strap-and-harness rear-mount rack each time you wash your car is a bother. I have used two models (Wild Side Designs and The Bike Slider) that simply slip out of a two-inch receiver hitch. With both I employ my U-lock to secure the bike and front wheel to the rigid, all-steel rack frame, and therefore when leaving the vehicle can feel far more at ease than with other rack designs. (See photo.) Extremely convenient in all respects, I prefer these hitch models to all others.

However, these racks are more expensive, and cars built low to the ground sometimes have problems with either the hitch or the relatively low-hanging bike wheels striking the ground. The point, of course, is that there are pros and cons with every model. Take your time in choosing one.

TOOLS/WORK STAND

Most commuters and weekend riders pack along a basic set of tools and re-placement parts, those which are necessary to fix the kinds of problems sometimes encountered on the road. Backcountry tours, far away from the emergency rooms and critical care wards of bike shops, will of course make riders carry a bit more gear.

The following is my personal tool list, and because I do not wish to change its composition constantly I pack along the same gear all the time—commuting, weekend trail rides, very long tours. Choose from my list carefully, therefore, to do away with unnecessary weight for your particular style of cy-cling. (For example, perhaps just a few allen wrenches, a small channel locks and screwdriver, tire levers and spare tube, brake/gear cable, and chain rivet tool for commuters. Trail riders who fear broken spokes should add a spoke wrench, spare spokes, freewheel remover, a pocket vise for non-cassette hubs, and a freewheel sprocket removal tool for cassette hubs. They might also add cone wrenches and a cotterless crank removal tool if the trail bashing will be great.)

1. Crescent wrench—6″

2. Channel locks—7″

3. Regular blade screwdriver (thin, lightweight, with short handle and slightly longer shank for fine tuning derailleur set screws)

4. Allen wrenches (one for *every* size allen head on your bike)

5. Cone wrenches

6. Tire levers

7. Chain rivet tool

8. Spoke nipple wrench

9. Freewheel tool

10. Pocket vise

    To my on-the-road tool kit I add the following for at-home repairs:

1. Crescent wrench—15″

2. Crescent wrench—4″

3. Vise grips

BAUER, BOB

4. Needle-nose pliers

5. Swiss Army Knife

6. Universal cotterless crank wrench

7. Universal cotterless crankarm puller

8. Universal adjustable cup tool

9. Lock ring/fixed cup bottom bracket tool

10. Freewheel sprocket tools

11. Third Hand brake tool

12. Sealed bearing tools/roller cam brake tool

Work Stand On the road there is little choice but to flip a bike on its back to do repairs. Unfortunately, we can become confused about which way to turn screws when working upside down. It's a minor problem, surely, but some of us with little mechanical aptitude need all the help we can get. And if you like working on your bike as much as I do, it's tough enough getting around to the chore without putting more difficulties in your path.

Luckily, good mountain bikes are so well constructed that they require amazingly little care. Resembling a sturdy Clydesdale much more than their sleek, brittle-boned, thin-tired thoroughbred cousins, the reliable all-terrain bike might well give you years of service without a flat or broken cable, and almost never a broken spoke. Learn how and when to lubricate, and a few points of preventive maintenance (see chapter 7), and chances are you'll never experience a bad breakdown.

You will, however, have to adjust your derailleur now and again. The beefy cables probably won't break, but they will stretch. And for this operation (a surprisingly easy one, as you'll learn), as for general bike and chain cleaning, it is easiest to work away while the bike is upright and the rear wheel is lifted free from the ground. The answer?—a work stand.

Least expensive of all alternatives is what bike shops call "display stands." These are simple, two-legged twisted pieces of steel which wrap around the down tube at one end, and support the bottom bracket at the other. Considerably more costly, and a world apart in working comfort, is the Blackburn Work-Stand. Its 360-degree rotating jaws hold both wheels off the ground, making tune-ups even easier. And the entire stand folds up to hide easily in an apartment closet.

Left: Blackburn WorkStand

3

Riding Technique

SOME TIME AGO, while laboring through Henry James' seemingly interminable novel *The Golden Bowl,* I heard a single-line critique of the author's style that has remained with me ever since, and comes to mind as I begin this chapter: "Nuance, nuance—nothing but nuance!"

Webster's defines the word as "a slight or delicate variation, a shade of difference." Nuance, therefore, describes perfectly the problem of discussing riding technique on a mountain bike. I can provide the basics of saddle position during climbs and descents, of pedal position when riding trails, of how to lift one's wheels across a waterbar or jump over a ditch. But only time on the bike will teach you the delicate handling techniques required in tough terrain.

I will, therefore, be brief. But let me first come clean with you about this topic: My love affair with mountain bikes came about and remains because of where they take me, *not* because of the skiing-on-two-wheels thrills which are, I think, the primary delight of so many fat-tire enthusiasts. Besides, as I said earlier, I seldom travel even the trails without a great deal of photographic equipment, and the weight and delicacy of such a load is hardly conducive to taking chances.

There are some moves, however, which even loaded off-road cyclists must learn to avoid bad spills, pinched tubes, dented rims. I will discuss them. But I have gone to the experts* for lessons in the harder moves. I have hit the trails

*Sarah Lloyd Bennett, bike shop mechanic, river runner, and soon-to-be graduate student; Brian Thurgood, owner/operator of "The Road Less Traveled" mountain bike touring company; Tim Metos, owner of Wild Rose Mountain Sports in Salt Lake City.

with three of them to watch their technique, photograph their saddle styles, and marvel at their ability to traverse terrain I wouldn't have attempted on a mule. Over the next few pages you have their pictures, and my paraphrases of their remarks. And they have my hearty thanks.

CLIMBING

The general movement of mountain bike frame geometry over the last two years—especially that of shorter chainstays which place the rider's weight more directly over the rear wheel—means easier climbing up steep roads and trails. But no matter which bike you own you'll benefit from a momentary analysis of body position during a climb.

   In essence, climbing on a mountain bike is a matter of power, endurance, and balance. If the hill is too steep or your legs and arms too weak, or if you are good for the burst but not aerobically fit for longer pulls, even the best of riding styles will not take you to the top. Conversely, power—the kind of full-body, anaerobic effort seldom required in thin-tire recreational cycling, and endurance—the ability to keep all systems going for long mountain climbs, serve only to *help* you win a summit. A poor riding style requires a great deal more effort to make it up a hill; a lousy riding style will soon have you walking your bike.

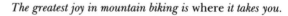

The greatest joy in mountain biking is where *it takes you.*

Why? Because the third ingredient—*balance*—is the key to transmitting that power and endurance into front-wheel contact and rear-wheel traction.

We all learned one kind of balance as kids, the kind required to keep us from falling off the bike to our right or left. The balance we need to discuss at present is in the other direction—forward and back. Simply, when going up a steep hill one must balance between the need for one's body weight to be over the rear wheel for traction, and the necessity to lean forward so as to hold the front end to the ground.

It seems plain enough: just keep the body in a straight line over the bike, lean forward for increased leg propulsion (granted by this crouched position) and to let some of your upper-torso weight assist the arms in keeping the front end down, and move your far greater body mass forward or back in the saddle as required for traction or front-end contact. That is, when you feel the rear wheel slipping a bit you know it requires more weight upon it; shift back a bit in the saddle. As the hill grows more steep and the front end tries to lift, you know it's time to apply weight there to keep it down.

Well, the *theory* is simple enough. But as with so many things the execution is far more complex. Especially, in this case, when the steepness of the hill appears to require your weight in both the front and rear at the same time. What can be done?

One option is to leave the saddle (not to walk; that's the last option, and we're not quite to it yet), to gain more power momentarily from the standing position and, by leaning forward, to hold the front end down. Tim Metos describes his technique as "scissoring"—using the body's far greater mass (five or six times that of the bike), and the momentum gained by standing up, to "lurch" the bike forward with the arms over a particularly steep section, then returning quickly to a sitting position if greater traction is required by the rear wheel.

Many more words can be written about this extremely important topic to mountain bikers, but you will learn the nuances far more quickly by spending your time in the saddle. I'll add only the suggestions that you outfit your bike with very low gears (as discussed in chapter 1), learn to anticipate the need to shift into a lower gear just *before* you begin straining at the pedals (derailleurs do not like being shifted at such high-torque moments, and respond sloppily), and realize that power, endurance, and balance are acquired only over time.

DESCENDING

Descents on a thin-tire bike are pure pleasure and little work; all you have to do is steer. On fat tires the pleasure is sometimes racheted upward to that of white-

Sarah demonstrating incorrect descent position: pedals should be parallel to ground and the body in a crouched position.

knuckled delight. Unfortunately, the work quotient is also increased—first by the hand and forearm strength required to slow one's speed to that approaching some degree of safety, and second by a need to apply those riding techniques necessary to keep from catapulting over the handlebars.

The first thing to learn before trying tough descents is which brake lever operates which brake. (The reason will become clear in a while.) Usually, but not always, the left lever works the front brake. Most of us learned years ago that it was a good idea while riding with hand brakes to apply both at the same time. Hit the brakes while riding down a steep hill on a bike (any bike) and you'll feel your body wanting to continue moving forward in the saddle; we intuitively use our arms and legs to counteract this tendency by pushing ourselves back in the saddle, and thereby keep the rear wheel on the ground. Mechanically the front brake is applying more stopping power; the rear brake is helping slow overall speed, as well as working with your backward body shift to keep your rear wheel and you from becoming airborne.

Now transfer this scenario to an *extremely* steep road or trail over rough terrain (when roads are paved they are usually made more moderate in grade by the engineers), and things become more complicated:

1. Maintain your normal, relatively upright/somewhat forward position in the saddle and you'll pitch over the bars.

Tim, "picking a line."

2. Fail to lower your saddle height (and thereby your center of gravity), or accomplish the same thing by dropping your rear end off the back of the saddle, and you'll pitch over the bars.

3. Attempt to steer laterally around an obstacle with your front brake locked as tightly as your rear brake and you'll pitch over the bars.

Sounds painful, huh? Well, so too is a bad flip off the high dive, a poorly executed telemark, and a not-quite-high-enough pole vault. They all take practice, and the before-hand smarts to start off small. I should also take this opportunity to point out the obvious fact that wearing a helmet at these times is a real must. (Two of our three experts saw fit to wrap their skulls in plastic before venturing forth. The unhelmeted third is simply exercising his right to think for himself, enjoy the wind through his hair, and die at an early age.)

    Back to technique. Notice that Sarah, in the photo on p. 64, has assumed the proper slightly-out-of-the-saddle, three-and-nine-o'clock pedal position necessary for a descent; keep one foot or the other close to the ground (six o'clock) and you stand a far better chance of it or the pedal striking an object, propelling you out of the saddle or at least off your chosen path. Tim, on this page, has assumed the same position (similar to that of a jockey in the stretch) and is "picking a line"—sitting up in the saddle to see far ahead and choosing his path

Position necessary for flying down a hill when seatpost has not been lowered.

of descent. You already know this technique if you run rivers—that exciting, apprehensive moment when you round the bend, focus on the rapids out ahead, and must choose your path over them.

On page 59 you see Tim going over a large rock in the descent. As he approached it he shifted his weight back in the saddle to let the unweighted front end climb easily up and over. If this were level terrain, he would have then shifted his weight forward to allow an unweighted rear end hop over the obstacle, thereby producing slight contact and avoiding a pinched tube or damage to the rim. On this steep descent, however (which by the way is much steeper than it appears in the photos), his weight must remain back in the saddle to counteract the grade. (Rear wheel damage is avoided by extremely slow speed.)

More important than body position, however, is what he's doing with the brakes. The rear is applied, but the front is being "feathered" (the same action one does with the gas pedal when trying to start a car on a very cold day), for locking it up will not only cause him to pitch forward but also deny him the ability to change directions right or left. (All three of the riders agreed that learning to "let go"—acquiring that speed necessary to roll over obstacles or change directions while descending—is one of the hardest techniques to master.)

Notice too that knees and elbows remain somewhat bent, to act as shock absorbers and allow more fluid movement. Another point: If it became obvious that gravity was winning out, Tim would have attempted to separate himself from the bike, dropping it beneath him preferably on the non-derailleur side and hopping off to safety.

The photo above shows Brian flying downhill in the position required if one doesn't take the time to lower the saddle. Remember that great skill is necessary to hang this far rearward and still steer safely.

By shifting his weight to the rear, Tim allows the unweighted front wheel to climb easily over the rock.

Knees and elbows are slightly bent to act as shock absorbers and allow more fluid movement.

Aggressive front tire.

Smooth-rolling rear tire.

Note: I happened to ask Tim about his preference in tires. He surprised me in responding that he likes riding with two different treads—a more aggressive tread in front, a tire which rolls better in the rear. His reasoning is that "The body tends to follow the front wheel, so if it washes out first and the back wheel hangs you tend to pitch around sideways. In this case the body starts leading the bike rather than the bike leading the body. If on the other hand the rear wheel washes out, you tend to hang on to the bars and are still following the bike, which is easy to correct."

Counter-balancing to avoid an obstacle.

Brian lifts front wheel; rear wheel rolls up and over curb.

AVOIDING OBSTACLES

On a dirt road or wide path the rider has the option of moving around an obstacle. On narrow single-tracks, however, they must be negotiated in other ways.

On page 60 Sarah is demonstrating avoidance by leaning the bike sharply away from the obstacle, and counter-balancing by leaning the body in the opposite direction.

But let's say the obstacle runs completely across the path, such as in the case of a waterbar. (Waterbars are earth or wooden trenches which funnel mountain runoff across a trail.) They often are raised many inches above the path surface, and will cause wheel damage or a fall if not negotiated carefully.)

Above, Brian has lifted his front wheel—the easiest option in crossing a waterbar (or in this case the very similar obstacle of a curb). Pedaling at slightly reduced speed to a point just before the curb, he has slid rearward in the saddle and, at the same time, lifted up on the bars and pushed them forward. The momentum thus gained allows his front wheel to become airborne over the curb; now the task is to move his rear wheel across with as little contact as possible. This is effected by a quick transference in body weight—once the front wheel is safely over—toward the front of the bike.

Tim performs a static jump.

A second technique for clearing across-the-path obstacles is similar to the wheelie, though the attempt here is to hop over without either wheel touching. In this case one requires a bit more speed, then almost the same moves as above. Once airborne, however, the body weight must be transferred forward even more dramatically and the handlebars pushed downward; the hoped-for reaction is for the rear wheel to soar over whatever is being jumped. Remember to keep the front wheel perfectly straight when hitting the ground, as an angled wheel can cause a bad spill.

Tim, seen above, shows the beginning move in a static jump, a method of crossing an obstacle when you haven't had the opportunity to gain momentum. Notice that he has compressed himself on the bike much as he might if begin-

Tim executes a moving leap.

ning to jump while standing: knees bent, body in a crouch, ready to spring upward.

On this page you see him executing a moving leap, again from a compressed position, but this time using the momentum of forward movement to help him pull the bike from the ground. His feet in the clips lift the rear of the bike; his hands lift the front end. (Notice the Hite Rite on Tim's bike in this picture.)

Note: On technical descents (i.e., downhill runs through rough terrain; see again Sarah's rough path on page 64), a hop is not an option to clear obstacles, as one must maintain contact with the ground.

Other obstacles must be negotiated with similar planning and skill. Narrow ditches can be jumped; wide, shallow ditches can be ridden straight across if the walls aren't steep, or at an angle if they are; wide, deep ditches act upon your bike and you as tank traps do on tanks. Be careful. And shallow streams can be crossed if taken at good speed, once you have reconnoitered them for depth, of course. (I assume that your sensitivity to the environment, as well as your desire not to increase the number of areas from which mountain bikes are excluded, means you are only riding streams at spots where they cross roads. I hope too that you aren't locking your rear wheel during descents in soft soils—thereby causing ruts, or chewing up fallen logs by bashing them with chainrings while attempting jumps. Much more on this in chapter 6.)

STARTING OFF ON A HILL

Any number of reasons can cause you to "lose" a hill, and if you don't know how to get started again, you will be spending a lot of time walking to the top. The following technique is especially useful when you've stopped on a steep grade. If you aren't already in a very low gear, move your shift lever a bit, lift the rear wheel and pedal with your other hand, and continue to do this until you manage to jump your chain into the proper sprockets.

On page 65 you can see Tim in the starting position: left foot on the

Hops are not an option on tough descents.

ground, right foot on the pedal, body leaning forward. He is rocking back and forth slightly, as one might on a swing to gain momentum, then simultaneously pushes off with the left leg and pushes down with the right.

The next photo shows the left leg rising to begin its search for the pedal, as the right leg continues its propulsion. If his left foot has not found the pedal by the time his right pedal reaches six o'clock, he'll have to stop and try again.

The shot taken a moment later shows the left foot very close to locating the left pedal. And then page 67 pictures Tim successfully in the clips and straps, standing in the pedals and leaning forward to increase momentum.

CARRYING THE BIKE

This is usually not an option for me. With all the weight I normally pack it's either ride or push. But chances are you will be pedaling a far lighter rig, and so should know how to portage.

Several companies offer "carry straps," "slings," and "pads" designed specifically for comfort when packing a bike along on your shoulder. When used, the bike's handlebars point in the same direction that one walks; the pedal is tucked either forward or back of the torso.

Many bikers don't care for pads that attach to the bike, as on some frames

Starting position for hill-climbing.

The left leg searches for the pedal as the right continues its propulsion.

The left foot locating the pedal.

they take up the space that could be occupied by a water bottle and are not needed for comfortable portaging.

Now you have plenty of information to begin your own trail work. Start off small, don't be impatient, but do be careful. And for heaven's sake (and your own), at least at first ride with a friend—preferably one who already knows the moves.

The left foot is in the clip and ready to pedal.

Tim uses his foot to push the left pedal into the nine o'clock position.

After hoisting the bike up by the top tube with his right hand, Tim reaches through the main frame triangle and grabs hold of the handlebars while his left hand holds the saddle.

The pedal is tucked to the side of the hip, the crank arm rests comfortably against the small of the back, and the top tube lies across the shoulders. In this position you can carry the bike easily for a great distance, as well as maneuver the bike's front and rear wheels around obstacles (through the control provided by your grip on both the saddle and the handlebars).

4

Urban Jungles

Present options in stylish (yet functional) clothing, and in footwear and foul weather gear, allow today's worker in almost any profession to ride to his or her job. It is already obvious that this mode of travel is healthier, extremely economical, and—believe me—fun. But what probably is *not* so easily seen is the personal satisfaction that comes from two-wheeled commuting.

No doubt at first the thought of rising a bit earlier each day, of taking on the elements and traffic and having to worry a bit with packing a shirt or blouse, will seem to be yet another bothersome task. But you aren't alone. Most of America's roughly two million bike commuters probably felt the same way at first, and probably, like you, began commuting for one of the reasons listed below. But they stay with it, many year-round, for those initial reasons—plus one: after everything else, it's fun.

Cycle commutation is economical, good exercise, and environmentally sound. It also gets us outside, and tunes us in every day to the natural world; think for a moment how much time you spend indoors (including your cross-town hours in a car), and what a pleasure it will be to engage nature so fully on a daily basis. Surely, cold days are more bitter, hot days hotter, and nights far blacker than when seen behind twin beams. But I can promise you that you'll appreciate the waiting coffee cup at work, and the first cool hint of coming autumn, far more when you have known their opposites. And although evening low-light commutes in winter require far more care, you will find there is something romantic about knowing each phase of the moon.

Commuting by bike is good exercise, economical, and it gets you outdoors.

If you aren't already very experienced at commuting by bike, for heaven's sake (and that of your skull's) approach this topic with respect. Most riders will think a bit before hitting the trails; they venture forth with a veteran who can teach them the moves, analyze their mistakes, and work up to fast descents on rough terrain. But this isn't the case with commuting. We throw ourselves into it with little forethought, no doubt because we're all so used to driving through this pandemonium. It's a wonder that most of us keep from getting creamed.

I wrote in my first (thin-tire) book many years ago: "All the savvy of an animal in the bush is necessary to negotiate a business district without winding up as a hood ornament. . . ." Mountain bikes are infinitely safer commuting machines than their spindly, unstable cousins, prone as they are to overreacting when they hit a pothole or piece of glass. But don't get cocky; ATBs and Buicks still aren't an even match.

A COMMUTER'S BIKE

I will provide only a quick checklist and some photographs here, as much has already been covered. But such a list, and the comparison of your bike with the two-wheeled urban animal pictured beneath the happy commuter, should help you in your preparations before the initial ride to work.

Upswept bars

Some cyclists prefer the head-up, traffic-watching position that these handle-bars allow. Perhaps if I planned only to commute I'd choose them, but we cross-over bikers (weekday commuters, weekend tourers/trail riders) do not find them as compatible as somewhat straighter bars in the wilds.

Rearview mirror

A must. As with many of the items listed here, various models are discussed in an earlier chapter.

Handlebar bell

This is the civilized way to communicate to pedestrians. Or you can blast them out of the way with a compressed-air horn. The disadvantage of the horn is that your ears also have to hear it, and chances are the next time you apply for a job your interviewer will be the man or woman you assaulted. (A second disadvantage is that some compressed-air horns lose their voices when temperatures run below freezing.) I do, however, suggest the horn for crisis communications with motorists, and especially for female commuters who must ride after dark.

Handlebar bell.

And while we're on the subject of communication, realize two things as you meet the streets on your maiden commute: First, you are not a car, and therefore should not act as one. And second, once a motorist does recognize that you're a human on a bike, and worthy of at least a second thought, your facial features and hand movements are much more visible than when you are sitting behind a wheel. The opportunity for *personal* communication—human to human, not bike to car—is greatly increased. Learn to use it to your advantage. A simple wave of thanks when you've been given the go-ahead, or a nodding *mea culpa* when you've pulled a bonehead move, will do much to make that motorist think kindly of the next cyclist who wanders into range.

Tires

I have already given my strong preference—the Specialized Crossroads II: skinwall, 1.95″ wide, variable pressure of 35–80 psi, an interlocking knobby pattern that allows one to run along on an unbroken bead of rubber when the tire is hard, yet grants excellent traction when deflated for dirt. Other choices (of many): the Avocet FasGrip City/K 1.9 (1.9″ wide, completely treadless, 45–80 psi); and, for real speed on long commutes, the CyclePro Streetster (1.5″, 100 psi). The Streetster, by the way, is Kevlar belted to protect against flats. Don't forget tire liners (like Mr. Tuffys) if you choose non-Kevlar rubber for your wheeling through glass-and-nail-infested city streets.

When you're pedaling snow and ice, IRC Tire Company offers a "Blizzard" model, complete with studs.

Fenders

The only ones I find sufficient to keep me from looking like a mudball are wide, full-wrap beauties front and rear. My favorite is the Mt. Zefal, for its longer reach in the rear, and with the self-applied addition of a pop-riveted mudflap in front.

Pedals

Start off with wide ones, to accept the lightweight boots you'll probably be wearing when inclement weather hits. Then add reflectors, and either half-clips for exclusive around-town use, or full-on clips and straps. If the clips are metal

Avocet FasGrip City K 1/9 and CyclePro Streetster.

IRC studded Blizzard.

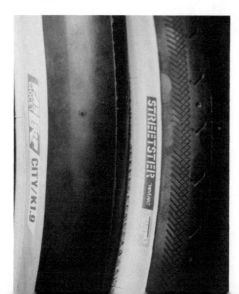

you might tape them to keep the toes of leather dress shoes from becoming scratched.

Gearing

Review remarks in earlier chapters on why I feel mountain bikes at present are poorly geared both for very tough climbs and fast pavement commutes. Fortunately, one's gear pattern can be changed.

Water bottle

I carry one filled with water on long commutes, and one filled with ammonia (or a can of HALT!) for rides which run a gauntlet of man's best friends. I'm not sure if these are still offered, but at one time thermoses (sized to fit a water bottle cage) were available—perfect for those of us who savor coffee beans as others adore the grape.

Racks

A rear rack will satisfy the needs of most commuters, but if you pack a lot to work and back (or decide to go shopping on your way home), you'll find a front rack convenient. (Again, see Chapter 2 for further discussion.)

Packs

I need add only this reminder to my earlier remarks: When buying a bag or bags which will ride with you always, make sure the attachment/detachment system is sufficiently quick and easy to allow repeated workings on a single ride home. Choose one that is difficult and you'll begin to leave it on your bike—which means you'll have the opportunity to buy another very soon.

Rain covers

Ponchos for bike bags. Buy them if you're interested in keeping your pannier contents dry.

Pump

Choose one short enough to fit inside (not stick out of, for this makes putting a pannier cover over the bag a pain) your ever-present commuting bag, or one that will attach to it. The alternative is to mount it on your bike, which means you have one more thing to carry away from the bike each time you stop.

Mixte frame.

Saddle

On some models (especially dyed leather) you will need to use a saddle cover to avoid staining pants, culottes, skirts (yes, skirts—one can ride in these without entertaining the world or causing accidents if on a "mixte" frame—the top tube runs somewhat parallel to the down tube, meaning there is nothing high to straddle).

Lights

Begin with pedal reflectors, and at least a large red reflector at the end of your rear rack. Now add the excellent flashing Belt Beacon (the battery lasts forever) and a headband lamp (the kind campers use when putting up tents after dark)—minimum requirements to be seen. You'll need more, however, if you wish to see where you are going. Take a look at the very bright Brite Lite rechargeable-battery system (and similar models), or the far less expensive (and much less illuminating) handlebar or stem-mounting battery models. And if you don't employ a kickstand, aren't set up with a chainstay-mounted U-brake, and ride with either slicks or interlocking knobs, you might investigate the chainstay/bottom-bracket-style generators. (On many tires the aggressive side knobs prevent the use of seatstay-mounted generators, whose metal friction wheels must engage the tire sidewall.)

Belt Beacon.

Locks

Review chapter 2's remarks on this all-important topic, then make sure you protect your seatpost and saddle with a Hite-Rite, Seat Leash, or replacement of your quick-release skewer, and your quick-release front wheel either with a second lock or by affixing it with the frame. (See photo.) A long-shackle lock, like the excellent Rhode Gear Citadel XL pictured, makes the locking of both the frame and front wheel (without having to remove the wheel) together a much easier task.

Packing a U-lock can be accomplished by hanging it from the saddle rails (impossible with some saddles), strapping it to a rack top, slipping it into a pannier or beneath the many "rack trunk" bags which have a special sleeve sewn in for them, or employing a Rhode Gear Snap-Lok Bracket.

Rhode Gear Citadel XL shows the advantage of a long shackle.

A COMMUTER'S DRESS

During the years that I spent teaching I usually rode to work in whatever pants and shirt I planned to teach in that day, and packed my tie and sport coat (folded once and slipped into a plastic bag, it fit nicely in a pannier and didn't wrinkle). On very warm days it took only a minute to fold my dress shirt as would a professional laundry, then pack it in a bike bag by itself; I then pedaled in a T-shirt and jettisoned the thing when reaching school.

Female commuters need not feel they are forced by biking into wearing pants. I have already mentioned the mixte frame for use when wearing a skirt, but the preference of many female commuters who prefer looking more feminine on occasion and to ride in what they'll wear at work is the delightfully functional and good-looking culotte. In essence these are short trousers, cut very full in the legs to resemble a skirt when one is standing. But when on a bike the woman is not impeded by the top tube.

Bike gloves

By all means, to avoid the black hand-grip discoloration, for comfort in the saddle, and protection if you fall. Padding at the heel of the hand is needed to avoid nerve compression at that point, which causes fingers to go numb. Read further comments in chapter 2.

Pants clips

Rubber bands work, but have the habit of breaking when you've just re-lubed your chain and are wearing your best slacks. You have your choice of metal bands, or fabric (oftentimes reflective for night travel) strips with a velcro patch to stay in place.

Pants protector

The "LeGuard" is a product I've used now only for a few months, and wish mightily I had owned more than a decade ago. Made of washable, durable coated nylon, the "LeGuard" wraps around the inside of the right leg to protect it from chain or chainring grease. Two velcro straps hold it firmly in place, and the entire lightweight guard folds up nicely to stow away in a pocket or be suspended from a belt. Use this in place of a pants clip on your right leg and you stand an excellent chance of spending far fewer dollars on dry-cleaning fees. (Address in Appendix.)

Poncho/chaps or rainsuit

Cyclists have two major choices when it comes to staying dry—the poncho/chaps combination, or a rainsuit. I use a rainsuit for mid-winter commutes, a poncho and chaps at all other times. This is because of the rainsuit's problem of heat buildup. No matter the material, pedal hard inside a suit and after a while you'll feel as if you're working out in a greenhouse. This makes them great when it's raining and the temperature is near the freezing point, but horrible when it's warm.

Bike ponchos, on the other hand, are designed to allow air to circulate around the body while still shedding rain. This works because of their unique design—pullover, tentlike, waterproof, with the back flap tying about the waist and the front with thumb loops to stretch this portion out to the handlebars. However, a hard or more horizontal rain (those days that remain in memory, when it comes in sheets blown by ferocious winds) can still soak one's lower torso. And this is where the chaps come in. (It is especially critical when commuting to have a poncho hood which can be drawn tightly around the face. If this isn't done, you will lose your peripheral vision, thereby greatly decreasing your chances of avoiding accidents. See further comments on rain-riding safety in the paragraph below on goggles.)

Pants clips.

Rain pants could be worn, but these close off the crotch and waist to airflow, causing dampness inside. Chaps, however, are simple waterproof tubes that tie at the waist to a beltloop, thereby allowing air to circulate. The chap bottoms overlap the gaiters (the shoe coverings discussed next), which in turn overlap the open portions of shoes or boots. It is a system similar to roof tiles, with successive, rain-shedding layers.

Note: Don't think you have to buy a new poncho/chaps outfit if yours begins to leak. The "K-Kote" waterproofing can be restored with products such as "Re-Kote" and "Flex-Dri," available in some outdoor shops and catalogues.

Poncho and gaiters.

Gaiters/rainboots

Designed to shed water away from the tops of one's boots or shoes, gaiters attach beneath the instep (with a strap) and to the laces (with a hook), and are usually zippered up the back or side, though front zippers (with covering flap) are my preference. I also prefer very long gaiters which reach just below the knee, for on most days these will shed almost all the rain that blows beneath your poncho, as well as protect you from roadsplash. Choose the more expensive, breathable fabrics for your gaiters and you won't find perspiration buildup at the ankles.

Shedding water downward from your poncho and gaiters (or poncho/chaps/gaiters in warm-weather storms, and rainsuit in winter) to a lightweight waterproofed boot (use Snow Seal, saddle soap, or other quality leather dressing) is fine if your dress shoes are waiting for you at work, or packed in a pannier. My personal system has always been to leave a pair at work, and ride with warm, stiff boots in winter, and lighter, cooler (but still stiff) low-cut shoes in warmer months.

However, if you prefer to pedal in your work shoes (excluding high heels) you will need to take several steps: (1) for good-weather commutes, wrap metal toe clips to avoid abrasions on good leather shoes, (2) obtain a pair of Spenco Orthotics (available in many bike shops) or other inserts to stiffen the midsole for efficient and comfortable pedaling, and (3) wear rain boots in foul weather. Very bad storms and heavy snows usually have me (on both commutes and tours) donning either a poncho/chaps/rain boots combination, or rain suit and rain boots, for I have yet to find a boot that is completely waterproof after an hour or so of being soaked. During the first of my dozen car-less years I had a thirty-mile roundtrip commute each day when teaching school in St. Louis. That distance, and a far wetter climate than my present arid West, taught me much about keeping dry.

Good rain boots are hard to find. I hesitate to suggest a single brand, as others may become available, but in just the past few months I have obtained a pair of Madden's (a Boulder, Colorado, pannier company) Hot Dogs!, made of heavy packcloth uppers and a very tough cordura soul. These rain boots are just too good not to mention.

Goggles

Normally my lightly-tinted Ambermatic sunglasses provide my eyes sufficient protection from the rain. But on days when it's pouring, and anytime at night, completely clear goggles are a necessity. This is yet another item usually not carried in bike shops, and therefore can be difficult to find. I now wear a brand called Kroop's Goggles (address in Appendix), for they are extremely light, have a leather binding, vent holes (to prevent fogging), very good sealing action against the elements (a result of the leather binding making close contact with the skin), and cost little. Be sure to pack them in some kind of cloth wrapping, as plastic lenses scratch easily.

And while we're in the wet, let me add that if you're goggled *you* can see the world about you better than most motorists. A motorist's task of seeing through his cocoon is tough. *Do not assume you're seen.* If it makes sense to drive defensively when you're behind the wheel, it is a must for continued life to ride in the same manner.

Gloves/stocking cap/face mask

I've found nothing better than large ski gloves for winter travel. I use a pair of very thin, high-cuff waterproof shells to keep my ski gloves dry in rain and snow. Spenco's new All Weather gloves have the normal bike-glove half-fingers, plus an attached mitten flap for use when it's cold. I think the unique design might warrant your interest.

Some riders like the one-piece stocking cap/face mask, but these freeze to my beard, and when commuting in a one-piece mask I'm always afraid I'll be mistaken for a bank robber. In addition, as a rule I wish as much of my cycle wear to perform more than one task, as they do when protecting one part of my body when worn alone, yet contributing to total protection when used in conjunction with other gear.

This principle is obvious in my choice of a wool or capilene* stocking cap which protects the head, and a neoprene face (or ski) mask which covers only the nose, mouth, cheeks, and chin, and is held in place behind the head with velcro.

Cool-weather riding cap

A stocking cap is perfect by itself or beneath a helmet for very cold weather, but in spring and autumn I prefer a cap that goes by several different names, and is therefore best described. Think of the dapper caps worn by drivers of foreign sports cars, when the tops are down. Usually they have a snap above the slight bill, and are aerodynamically shaped to handle the wind—by sloping downward in front. I find that such a cap, if it fits rather tight, will remain on my head despite passing traffic and headwinds.

---

*Capilene is an excellent fabric for wicking moisture away from the skin, and is far better than poly-propylene—especially for long underwear—in remaining odor free and supple.

Jacket/vest

The principle of 'layering' is known to most outdoor sports enthusiasts. A heavy single coat will feel good for the first few blocks of your commute, but far too hot after that. Your only options are to unzip the thing (in which case your arms and back will remain too warm and soon be wet with perspiration), or remove it completely and freeze.

By donning layers of clothes one can easily and quickly adjust to changes in the weather and the physical demands of the ride. In winter I begin with two-piece capilene long underwear, then my normal shirt and slacks, and top off with a lightweight jacket of a nylon outer shell (to repel wind) and capilene insulation. On coldest days I add a thick vest of Quallofil or other man-made fabric.

Kroop's goggles.

5

Backcountry Touring

I NEEDN'T SPEND much time selling you on touring in the backcountry. Chances are you'll come to the thought soon enough, when at the end of a wonderful day ride you deplore the thought of going home. The question really is not why to tour, but *how*.

This chapter is designed to answer the basic queries—what gear to take, how to pack it, how it will affect the ride—and to help you choose the best route and get you home again (through a quick lesson in reading topos), and to suggest that what is almost universally perceived as cycle touring—tents, sleeping bags, God-awful weight and lots of work—is tunnel vision at its worst. Most people think of touring as a night spent on the road. Well, *where* you spend that night is up to you. I've passed them trapped in my tent by Colorado snow at twelve thousand feet, and in romantic Vermont bed-and-breakfast inns. Both times I was touring—and enjoying it immensely.

This is not simply a plug for another of my books, but if you wish to delve far more deeply into the topic of cycle touring than we have the space for here, allow me to suggest *Touring on Two Wheels*. It is designed primarily for a thin-tire audience, but most of the data is appropriate for fat tires as well. I will therefore provide the following information (some of which is borrowed from my earlier title) on those critical topics in the most common form of touring (nighttime shelter on camping tours), offer an equipment checklist and a bit more data on your choice of stoves, and direct you to my far more extensive book on the subject if questions remain.

Little did I know when I pedaled into the dusty burg of Oatman, AZ, that while grabbing lunch in a bar, two burros were inspecting my gear for their own meal. Just one more reason for mountain bike bags to be tough.

SHELTER AND BEDDING

Tent

Begin searching for the perfect tent and you'll soon find we live in a complex world. So many choices! One-man tents, two-man tents, tents to fit a group; three-season and four-season models; freestanding or pegged; bivy sacks for simple shelter . . . the list goes on. I'll attempt to make it understandable, but you should once again prepare yourself for a lengthy search.

Naturally, you want a tent that is light, stable when erected, easy to put up and disassemble, of sufficient size, waterproof, and durable. As with bikes, unfortunately, such qualities come at a cost. Begin your search with an in-person, close-up look at some name-brand tents: Moss (not the only good tent around, but a company unbeaten when it comes to innovative designs and overall quality, and the one I've used exclusively for years, except for short-term tests of other brands), North Face, Bibler, Sierra Designs—compare the seams, stitching, fabrics, webbing, zippers, design, and poles with less expensive models. Give some thought to how much use you'll give it (it helps to think in terms of nights per year), and consider if long-term value makes the cost worth while.

Tents should be light, stable, and easy to erect.

Weight is a critical factor for cyclists, especially when one is contemplating a solo tour. (The load can be shared when there are more riders.) I'm speaking in the most general of terms, but for winter touring I try to keep my tent weight around four and a half pounds; for all other times, not much more than three. This would be relatively easy to accomplish if I weren't so completely sold on "self-supported" (freestanding) tents—those requiring no stakes to stand upright. The necessary cross-structure of poles on these tents increases their weight considerably. Self-supporters are much faster to erect (a consideration when it's about to rain), and, of course, can be used *inside* other shelter. This is done in such cases as barns and unheated garages, when warming the relatively small airspace of a tent makes sense.

I normally suggest that a person buy what's called a three-season tent (with large screened areas for airflow), and just tough it out in winter. Four-season tents are heavier, and I don't like packing the extra weight. Besides, a good pad and sleeping bag will get you through.

For summer desert travel I prefer almost completely screened tents. These are of course much lighter, but still heavy when compared to bivys. The word comes from "bivouac"—"a temporary encampment in the open, with only tents or improvised shelter"—and refers to the close-fitting sacks that serve as bug-proof, water-*resistant* sleeping bag liners. I stress "resistant," rather than water*proof,* because, whatever the fabric, I have yet to sleep completely dry in a bivy when it rains. A savings of weight, a great loss of comfort. Once more it is a question of balance that only you can decide, but not until you have a good idea of the kind of touring you have ahead.

Bivys have a problem of condensation due to their single "wall"—one piece of fabric between the occupant and the outside. Some of the more expensive models are made of Gore-tex, improving the bivy's breathability and thereby reducing moisture inside. Tents avoid much of this problem through a rain fly, a second "wall" that is waterproof, but suspended above the porous inner tent wall. Water vapor escapes through the first, then evaporates or con-

Bivy sack.

denses on the underside of the fly. With some experimentation you'll learn how much airflow is necessary inside the tent to prevent almost all condensation.

Tent size is an important consideration, especially if your tour is longer than a weekend. You'll find that all "two-man" tents are not the same size, so pay attention to the measurements given. As you did when choosing a bike, obtain catalogues and specification sheets for some deliberate, unrushed comparisons at home. Let me just add that for warm touring I pack a one-man tent; cool- and cold-weather rides bring out my two-man model—even when I'm riding solo. Why? Because of the extra gear I pack in cold weather, and because of the extra hours I'll be spending in the thing. The sun goes down very early in December, and rises late. And all those hours (once the cold has driven me from my campfire) I'm inside, reading by candlelight. At such times a little room, and a lot of comfort, are appreciated.

A few suggestions: Needle holes in fabric allow moisture to follow the threads inside. Be sure, therefore, to seal your seams. (A few tents come with a tube of such sealant; outdoor sporting goods stores and catalogues also carry it.) Some tourers carry a "ground sheet" to protect their tent floor from rocks and twigs; I choose to spend an extra minute combing the site for these objects, and leave the extra weight at home. Forget about tarpaulins. Some riders (especially those who have never weathered a storm or insect infestation in them) suggest these simple sheets of protection as an answer to the high cost of tents. Well, you get what you pay for. Rain and bugs fly in both ends, and putting up a tarp so that it won't flap about in the breeze is a real trick.

Six inches of ripstop repair tape is good to have along, to prevent any fabric rips from becoming larger. Finally, put your tent up at home a few times before you hit the road. Your first night's idyllic camp shouldn't be ruined by the realization that you're missing half the poles.

Sleeping bag

Skimp on most items for touring and you can, with a bit greater effort, overcome the problems that result. But when the sun goes down and you crawl inside a crummy bag, all you can do is shiver.

The "proper" bag for a ride is therefore crucial. I carry a very lightweight, semi-rectangular model for summer touring ("comfort-rated" at forty-five degrees), and a modified mummy minus-five-degrees heavyweight on winter rides. Now let's go over those terms.

Many riders at first think only in terms of temperature when it comes to bags. It's not a bad place to start, but don't stop there. Other considerations are shape (rectangular, semi-rectangular, modified mummy, mummy), kind of fill (or insulation—down, man-made), loft (the comfort- and warmth-producing thickness of insulation), construction (sideblock baffles, differential cuts, single layers, double layer offsets, zipper draft flaps . . .), and overall weight. Let us go into each of these primary considerations, but only so far as is necessary to choose wisely. After all, you're looking to buy a bag, not build it.

Shape: Think for a moment of what actually keeps you warm in a sleeping bag. Your body burns the fuel fed it throughout the day, maintaining its normal operating temperature. You give off some of this heat; the purpose of a sleeping bag (or bed cover at home) is simply to trap it, while keeping out the cold and at the same time allowing water vapor emitted by the body to escape. If this last point wasn't a problem, we could simply enclose a thick bag in a plastic sheathing and stay warm. Unfortunately, we'd wake up soaked in sweat.

A bag's shape is one of the critical elements in keeping the warmed air around you and the cold air out. The problem with rectangular bags is, first, that it's impossible to pull the top of the bag around your neck and shoulders sufficiently to retain warmth, and, second, that your body must work harder to warm the large airspaces created by that extra room.

You will recall that I pack a semi-rectangular bag in summer. This shape is tapered toward the foot (reducing airspace), yet still squared off at the top. On warm nights I can therefore adjust the amount of airflow for comfort; if there's a cold snap I can bundle up in clothing and still sleep pretty warm.

A modified mummy is tapered at the foot and closer about the shoulders than the semi-rectangular bag. In addition, the top is rounded to allow a close fit about the head—the spot from which we lose an amazing amount of body heat, because of blood flow to the brain, face, and scalp. Full mummies, the warmest of shapes, are body-contoured throughout. But I find them far less comfortable for sleeping than are the modified mummies, because rolling over in the things is difficult.

Fill: I would carry a down bag if I could be sure I'd keep it dry, if it were not so difficult to launder, and, finally, if the cost were more moderate. No man-made insulation is quite so compressible, quite so warm, or quite so good at maintaining loft (height of the insulating material in the bag).

But given these severe limitations, and the great advances over the last decade in man-made fills, I never pack down bags for touring. Remaining choices are Polarguard, Hollofil II, Polysoft fiberfil, Quallofil. . . . I can't guarantee I'd know the difference if I slept in them blindfolded, but for my winter bag I've chosen Quallofil. It is supposed to be ninety-five percent as compressible as down, excellent at maintaining loft (due to the anatomy of its "tubes"), and it retains ninety percent of its insulation capability even when wet (some companies claim ninety-five percent; down *loses* all but ten percent of its insulation capabilities when wet.).

Remember that most man-made fills can be machine-laundered and dried, without fears of "clumping" as with down.

Loft: This refers to the height of the insulating material in the bag. The greater the loft, the greater the dead air space between you and the cold, thus providing increased warmth. Down has amazingly good loft; I find Quallofil very good as well. You can help this by storing your bag according to directions, which means *not* leaving it crammed inside its stuff sack while at home. Several commercial products are available that guarantee improved loft if used when laundering a bag (such as REI Loft II). I must admit to having never used them.

It should be obvious that a thicker bag is more comfortable, as well as warmer. Keep this in mind when assessing the importance of loft.

Cosntruction: There's nothing mysterious about "offset quilting" and "shingled layers" when it comes to how a bag is made, but I can't see any sense in explaining each technique, especially since I'm not considering down. (With down's propensity for "cold spots," construction is more critical.) When I'm shopping for name-brand bags I pay more attention to loft and comfort rating, and assume the construction is all right.

However, no matter who the manufacturer is, I *always* look for what's called a "zipper draft flap" or "insulated draft tube"—a protective piece of insulation to prevent heat loss at the zipper junction. I also make sure the zipper has large tabs (or handles, to be found easily at night), does not bind or get caught easily in surrounding fabric when closed, and is of good quality (YKK is one very good and popular zipper brand). For those of you who will be traveling with a partner, be sure to buy bags with right or left zipper openings, so that two bags can be zipped together for a warmer sleep. Finally, the draw cord (at the shoulders on a semi-rectangular, around the head on modified and mummy) should be placed conveniently, operate smoothly, and come equipped with an easily released lock.

Overall weight: Don't get confused by "fill weights" when looking at the specifications of sleeping bags. That term refers to just what it says—the weight of the insulation only. It is an important consideration, especially when comparing bags. But what you'll feel while pedaling is found in the "total weight" column.

My summer bag is light—barely over two pounds. My winter sack tips in at about four pounds, eight ounces. That is heavy, making my shelter and bedding load almost ten pounds by itself. But when it's December, at night, in the cold, I don't begrudge an ounce.

Ground pad

A good pad is a necessary part of your attempt to have a good, restful sleep. In cold weather it insulates your bag from freezing, wet ground. And at any time of year it is far more comfortable than hard earth.

I find the most comfortable pads are the relatively heavy air mattresses. I'm not referring to the kind you take to the beach, but the well-made ones like Therm-A-Rest, with an air chamber *and* foam for comfort and warmth, all surrounded by a puncture-resistant nylon skin. Unlike the solid, nearly indestructible closed-cell ensolite foam pads, however, these can be damaged.

At about one-half the weight, and a quarter the cost, closed-cell foam pads are the popular alternative to air mattresses. Excellent at insulating the sleeper from the ground (though not quite so good as air mattresses), the closed-cell pads are far less comfortable. I've never found it difficult to sleep due to discomfort from the ground, but you might borrow someone's pad and try it before you buy.

Open-cell pads also exist, and are much softer (and therefore more comfortable) than closed cell kinds. However, they also insulate less well, weigh a bit more, and damage far more easily.

Beyond construction, you must decide upon pad length. "Regular" length is about five feet, leaving either your head or feet hanging over the end. "Long" pads are about six feet in length, and thus insulate a person more fully from the ground. It seems an obvious choice, at least in cold weather. But that extra foot of pad adds up to between a third and half a pound. I normally pack the shorter pad and simply insulate my head or feet with clothing.

FOOD FOR THE TOUR

Many thin-tire tourers, anxious to save on weight and usually not more than a couple of hours from a store or cafe, decide against packing a stove. I do quite well on most paved tours with my usual always-in-the-pannier complement of peanut butter, bread, jam, and cheese, supplemented daily by store purchases of fresh fruit and candy bars, and the trips to local cafes.

But things are different in the backcountry, especially when one is planning rides away from towns for days and days. In warmer seasons and in terrain that I anticipate will offer fuel I still forego a stove, simply to save the weight. But in early spring, late fall, and all the time in winter I add the ounces to my load. When the wood is wet, or I'm too tired (read lazy) to build a fire, there's nothing to beat producing BTUs with the flick of a match.

What does one cook? I start the evening meal, and end it, with instant coffee. In between I boil a couple cups of water, throw in two handfuls of "enriched, pre-cooked" Minute Rice, sprinkle half a box of Knorr's Soup and some jerky into the concoction, and roughly five minutes later am chowing down.

Breakfast is usually granola, over which I pour powdered milk, then add water and stir. The stove is cranked up only for coffee, or hot oats (liberally impregnated with raisins) if the temperature is in the teens and the skies are promising snow.

This leaves only lunch, and the twenty or so snack breaks between sun-up and when I blow my candle lantern to bed. Midday meals are always uncooked, unless it's been a wet and sloppy ride and suddenly I've spied a dry, inviting rock overhang. But usually it's peanut butter, jam, bread, and cheese, or sage rubbed between the hands and sprinkled over the peanut butter when the jam is gone. Snacks are anything I happened to have a fancy for the last day before the ride, and threw liberally into the bike bags. But almost always they are filled with goodly quantities of dried fruit and jerky. (Notes: (1) Pack your peanut butter and jam, and *especially* any honey, in high-quality plastic screw-lid jars. I've yet to meet a snap-lock lid that can handle a bike ride. (2) You'll save yourself a lot of money in the long run if you, and perhaps some biking/hiking friends, invest in a dehydrator. They're great for deer, elk, and beef jerky, and will expand your menu of dried fruits far beyond that offered by even the best-stocked health stores. (3) Do *not* keep food, or bags or clothing impregnated with the smell of food, in your tent overnight when you're in bear country. Pack a shank of parachute cord or very lightweight rope and suspend these items in a sack at least ten feet off the ground.)

Stoves

The "big three" factors when one considers a stove are type of fuel, weight, and cost. In the first of these categories the choice comes down to butane, white gas (Coleman or similar brands), and multifuel stoves (they burn white gas, kerosene, and sometimes alcohol). There are pros and cons in all corners.

Butane is by far the most convenient, for the fuel comes in canisters that are simply plugged into the stove and fired up—no priming or pumping required.

Disadvantages are the extreme high cost compared to white gas (roughly nine dollars per pound versus seventy cents), slightly poorer availability of canisters, the need to keep the canisters warm in winter (I put one in my sleeping bag at night), and the fact that they must be packed out even when empty (empty canisters weigh about 2½ ounces, full ones 8½ ounces).

White-gas stoves have to be pumped. I find this an extremely minor chore requiring, usually, only a few seconds. Preheating is necessary with some, but this involves merely the burning of a flammable paste along an inlet tube or the firing of a small pan of gas. I have found that these workhorses boil water faster than butane does. Fuel is plentiful and cheap throughout the United States and

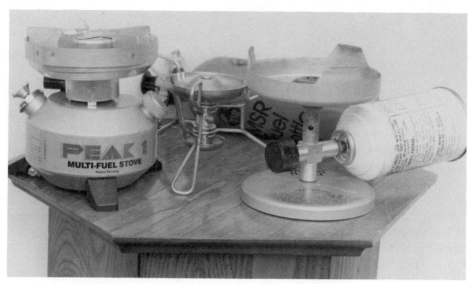

Camp stoves (left to right: Coleman Peak 1, MSR Whisperlite, Roberts).

Canada, but less available overseas.

Multifuel stoves are the most recent entries into the market, and make for a wise choice if you anticipate traveling abroad. But I suggest you use white gas when it is available. Kerosene is oily (spills will not evaporate quickly) and has an unpleasant smell; alcohol burns only half as hot as white gas and butane.

Most of my personal experience has come with the Hank Roberts (butane), an MSR WhisperLite and Coleman Peak 1 (white gas), and the Coleman Peak 1 Multi-Fuel (white gas and kerosene). I can recommend all these as excellent stoves—they have given me long and true service. However, in my opinion the early model Coleman is just too heavy for cycling; the Multi-Fuel model is a full third lighter.

Concerning the category of cost, I will leave that up to you and your Yellow Pages, except to say that you will probably find the Roberts by far the least expensive (until you buy fuel, of course).

I carry my WhisperLite or one of the Colemans inside the two-part aluminum Coleman "Cook Kit." The larger "pot" serves in the morning for my hot or cold cereal, in the evening for my rice/soup/jerky concoction; the smaller holds coffee always. When there's no cafe nearby and none in sight for days, it is heaven to roll out of the sleeping bag and fire up warm food. You'll have to pay for the pleasure in increased weight (nineteen ounces, empty, for both the MSR WhisperLite—with external fuel bottle—and Coleman Peak 1 Multi-Fuel; Hank Roberts weighs about eight ounces without cannister), but sometimes it's worth it.

All stoves provide the warning in their operating instructions. Even so, I'll add it here: Do *not* operate any model stove inside a closed tent or too close to the wall or roof. Not only might you have to re-shingle when the flame flares unpredictably, but you might not live to do so. Carbon monoxide is a by-product with every stove; good ventilation is a must.

EQUIPMENT CHECKLIST

What follows is the gear I pack on long tours, in regions of great elevation diversity and/or at those times of year when the weather might change quickly. Modify it to your own preferences, tailor it depending upon length and season of ride. But let me leave you with this thought before we begin the particulars—a personal motto, if you will, that applies to the whole of packing for a trip: "Go prepared for anything, and then enjoy it all."

Clothing for General Use

T-shirts (3)
Long-sleeved shirt (1) Most often I choose a lightweight, cotton Patagonia
   pullover sweatshirt.
Riding shorts (2) My strong personal favorite for any kind of cycling—
   Sportif 6-Pocket Espa Shorts (*not* the Sportif patch-pocket model made
   for cyclists).
Belt (1) Web, zippered compartment for money, hard plastic adjustable
   buckle for weight loss adjustments and for use as emergency sling.
Undershorts (3)
Long pants (1)
Gym shorts (1)
Insulated underwear (1 pair) I suggested Capilene above.
Leggings (1) Washable wool Protogs.
Socks (3 pairs)
Riding shoes (1 pair)
Camp moccasins (1 pair)
Bandanas (2)
Riding gloves (1 pair)
Riding cap (1)

Foul- and Cold-Weather Gear

Boots (1 pair) Stiff, lightweight hiking boots, or a high-top bike boot if the
   sole is sufficiently aggressive for pushing in the snow and mud.
Rain boots (1 pair)
Gaiters (1 pair)
Neck gaiter or scarf (1) Only for most bitter weather.
Rain chaps (1 pair)
Poncho (1)

Rainsuit (1) In place of poncho on mid-winter tours.

Goggles (1)

Gloves (2 pairs) Lightweight pair for warmer days; warmest gloves for days that start with hoarfrost fields and end with ice-draped tents.

Overmitts (1 pair) Long-cuffed waterproof shells, to counteract the effects of wind in cold weather—"wind-chill."

Face mask (1)

Stocking cap (1)

Jacket (1)

Vest (1)

Toe covers (2) Cordura covers which fit over the toeclips to serve as your first-line defense against cold feet.

Shelter and bedding

Tent (1)

Sleeping bag (1)

Ground pad (1)

Personal items

Towel (1) Small, thin hand towel.

Washcloth (1)

Soap (1 bar or bottle) Biodegradable—without exception.

Soap dish (1)

Toothbrush (1)

Toothbrush case (1)

Toothpaste (1 tube) Plastic tube or powder only; metal tubes crack.

Comb (1)

Toilet paper (partial roll)

Deodorant (1)

Shampoo (1)

Waterless hand cleaner (1)

Nailbrush (1)

Fingernail clipper (1)

Medical supplies

Sunshade (1)

Aspirin (20) Packed in cotton in a 35mm film canister, to avoid having them turn into white dust.

Snakebite kit (1)

Desitin (1) An antiseptic cream which I find better than all the rest in relieving the pain of sunburn and abrasion. Again, one 35mm container.

Band-Aids (10)

Butterfly closure bandages (6) Of various sizes.

Gauze compress pads (6) 4″ × 4″, in ziplock bag.

Gauze (1 roll)

Ace bandage/Spenco joint wraps (2)

Benadryl (1 package) An antihistamine to guard against allergic reactions.

Insect repellent (1 bottle)

Water-purification tablets (1 bottle), or purifier (1) Known for some time now as the "backpacker's bane," *Giardia lamblia*—a waterborne parasite that begins its life cycle when swallowed, and one to four weeks later has its host bloated, vomiting, shivering with chills and living in the bathroom—unfortunately will attack bikers as well. Discovered by Anton van Leeuwenhoek in 1681, the disease is known by most today simply as Giardia, and is avoided by boiling (the germs are killed almost at once when the temperature reaches 176 degrees), the addition of tetraglycine hydroperiodide tablets (sold under the names of Potable Aqua, Globaline, and Coughlan's) which impart a mild iodine taste, or by filtration through a water purifier. For its low cost and fast action I prefer the General Ecology "First-Need" purifier.

Moleskin/Spenco "Second Skin" (1 pad)

Tools and spare parts

(See chapter 7 for discussion of each item)

Crescent wrench (1) Six-inch adjustable.

Screwdriver (1) Regular (flat) blade, blade tip ³⁄₁₆″ wide, overall length six inches.

Channel locks (1) Seven-inch.

Tire levers (2)

Allen wrenches (As many as are required to fit *every* allen-head bolt on your bike.)

Cone wrenches (2)

Chain rivet tool (1)

Spoke nipple wrench (1)

Freewheel tool (1)

Pocket vise (1) Or a ten-millimeter hex wrench for the removal of cassette freewheels; or a freewheel cog removal tool; see chapter 7.

Cotterless crank removal tool (1)

Tube (1)

Tube repair kit (1)

Oil (1 bottle)

Grease (1 35mm film canister full)

Air pump (1)

Air gauge (1)

Brake cable/Gear cable (1)

Chain links (3)

Spokes (5)

Rack mounting bolts (2)

Rack straps (determined by load)

Miscellaneous

Pocket knife (1)

Sunglasses/case (1)

Flashlight/batteries (1). A cordless head lamp (powered by two AA batteries) is of immense help in erecting a tent in the dark.

Camera/film (1)

Rope (15') Parachute cord, or very thin nylon braid. Good for suspending food in bear country, as a clothesline, emergency shock cord, snare . . . .

Ripstop repair tape (6") Serves as a band-aid for your tent.

Matches (1 box) Large kitchen matches, their length trimmed to allow packing in a waterproof film canister.

Notebook (1)

Book (1)

Pen (1)

Safety pins (10) Various sizes.

Sewing kit (1)

Cup (1) If I'm not packing a stove and the Coleman cook kit, my metal Sierra Club cup serves as soup pot/coffee cup/oatmeal bowl over the open fire. If I am carrying the stove/cook kit I substitute a heavy duty Lexan plastic cup for the Sierra Club model, for I can then drink my coffee without burning my lips on the metal.

Utensil set (1 set) Lexan plastic, carried in its own bag to avoid contamina-

A good compass—like this Brunton model—is sometimes necessary for back roads and trail riding.

tion, and washed (as are the cup and cook kit) in the multi-purpose biodegradable soap, then rinsed well.

Can opener (1) G.I. style.

Pants clips (2)

Map (1)

Compass (1) On pavement tours one can usually count on road signs. On backcountry rides you must be able to provide your own guidance.

Candle lantern (1) The simple metal/glass globe lantern is the best system yet for winter reading in a tent. Dripless candles burn brightly for eight or nine hours, and the lantern itself weighs only five ounces in aluminum. I bought the slightly heavier brass one, however, for its beauty.

Candles (2) I sometimes lug along as many as eight, depending upon the season and my chance for resupply.

Watch (.1) Sometimes worn on pavement tours, seldom on backcountry rides.

Trowel (1) Often sold as the "backpacker's shovel," these are a necessity for burying human waste. Dig a cathole (nine or so inches deep), fire the paper, then cover all with dirt and tramp down. This "bury-and-burn" technique is little trouble for the health and aesthetic benefit. (Animals will sometimes dig up wastes, and thus expose unburned paper to dry in the sun and blow about the forest or woods. Be sure that the paper is burned completely and all fire is extinguished before you cover with dirt.)

LOADING/RIDING

Load distribution on a thin-tire bike is simple:

1.   Weight should be relatively even on either side.

2.   Weight should be distributed between the front and rear of the bike, in roughly a one-third/two-thirds proportion.

3.   Whenever possible, weight should be carried low and close to the frame.

For myself, the rules for loading an ATB are even easier to recall:

1.   Load the mountain bike as if it had thin tires.

Unfortunately, we can't stop there, for loaded touring on dirt roads and trails is a world apart from pedaling pavement. I have on occasion had to shift some of the items from front to back, when encountering terrain that required more inventive handling than is allowed by a heavily laden front end. Mountain

When loading an ATB, distribute weight evenly, keeping the weight low and close to the frame.

Schwinn Air-Dyne.

bike touring (especially my very weighty winter rides) forced me several years ago into far more upper-torso training than is necessary for pavement (I suggest rowing machines, weights, or the excellent *full-body* workout provided by the Schwinn Air-Dyne exercycle, followed of course by a good regimen of stretches to complete the physical fitness triad—strength, endurance, flexibility), but even this has not been sufficient to make handlebar wrestling on rough surfaces an agreeable day-long task. In short, one is risking spokes and rear-wheel rim damage, but you may find a one-quarter/three-quarters weight distribution to be the only workable proportion.

Some riders in fact say they prefer their touring weight in a backpack when riding single tracks. Well, maybe. But my first cross-country tour, a seventeen-hundred-mile ride aboard a three-speed in 1965, was done beneath a backpack. And then came three years of the Army. You will, I hope, understand that all I want on me now and in the future, whether hiking trails or single tracks on an ATB, is a very light day pack. It's been almost a quarter-century since I rode with heavy touring weight on my shoulders, but I would almost bet that even though one's bare bike *would* of course handle beautifully, you would soon be far too miserable to notice.

Work up to riding loaded. Take it a bit at a time, giving upper- and lower-torso muscles, and your rear end, a chance to condition themselves to the change.

Now for some specific "gear location" and other tips:

1.   You'll need your compass a lot in the wilds. Keep it—and your snakebite kit—in the handlebar bag, where you can reach them quickly.

2.   Purchase a seat bag (under-the-saddle bag) large enough to hold at least your poncho, the first item you'll want to don when there's a storm. If possible keep your chaps and saddle cover there as well. Next in rainwear, I house all my pannier covers in a single bag, preferably along with my rain boots. This way there is but a single zipper to work, not four or five. Seconds count when attempting to keep dry, and this way you're opening only one bag to the drops.

3.   Tent, sleeping bag, and ground pad for me always ride perpendicular to and on the rear rack. As the tent is usually the heaviest of these items it rides forward of the sleeping bag on the rack; the ground pad rests on top, between the two.

Seat bag.

4. Regular bread is enough of a pain to keep from smashing on thin-tire tours; it's next to impossible to keep from mangling on an ATB. The flat "pocket" bread is a good alternative, and bagels are great for everything but peanut butter and jam. Also, get in the habit of packing food on the derailleur side of the bike, and add it to the habit of laying the bike down always on the non-derailleur side.

5. As suggested earlier, carry peanut butter, jam, honey, and any similar items in high-quality, screw-lid plastic jars. Also pack all fresh fruit in plastic bags. Even the hardest pear will develop bruises after the first few miles; after ten it will get revenge by smearing itself all over your bike bag.

6. Fail to follow any of the five suggestions above and the result might be a minor nuisance. But *this* is critical: large items usually carried outside the panniers (and therefore unprotected by waterproof bag covers)—tent, sleeping bag, ground pad on the rear rack, jacket and vest (when I'm on tour) on the front rack—must be in absolutely waterproof stuff sacks. On mid-winter tours I even double-sack my sleeping bag, just to be sure. You'll shudder when you see how much good stuff sacks cost, but get these items soaked in cold weather, or in high summer when you're in the desert, and you'll wish you'd spent the bucks. (I seal my stuff sack seams just like my tent.)

UNLOADED TOURING

Sounds great, doesn't it, especially after all the "heavy" talk above? By far the majority of all-terrain tourers seem to prefer it, packing only tools and a change of underwear along with their credit cards. Riding unburdened toward a warm shower, white tablecloths and clean sheets just can't be beat. I love it for itself, and *also* for the stark contrast that it provides from all my other touring. Try not to fall into the "either-or" school of tourers, at least until you've given each a chance.

But a few minutes' thought on "unloaded" touring should have you thinking in specifics. "What is a safe minimum to carry?" "What if there's a breakdown?" "What if there's a storm?"

You will need all the tools and replacement parts, (spare tube, tube repair kit, spokes, gear/brake cable, air pump . . .), listed earlier of course. Beyond that, *even when I'm riding toward confirmed reservations,* I pack along what I think the season and terrain will require to get me through the night. That is, what is necessary to let me survive a night out in the open, not pass it comfortably. Now, if it's late spring through early fall in the Midwest, chances are the temperature drop at night will not be such to cause any worry. But where I live, in the alpine regions and high deserts of the West, things can get mighty cool in any month.

One is seldom more than fifteen or twenty miles from civilization, or a road toward it, on day rides. But when packing light and planning to stay inside, many cyclists double or even triple this mileage on good dirt roads. (I have many times mountain biked more than a hundred miles in a day on pavement. But I prefer to cut this back *at least* by half on good dirt roads, and by half again on tough jeep roads and trails.) The point is that as one's intended backcountry mileage increases due to a light bike and overnights inside, so do the risks of breakdowns in between.

I pack all my usual tools and replacement parts, my normal complement of medical supplies, a set of long underwear and a bivy. The first category of items will guard against bike breakdowns, the second against breakdowns of my body. The long underwear and bivy sack in combination will help me through the night, especially the latter if I can't find a spot out of the snow or rain. If you don't own a bivy I suggest you pack along at least a lightweight, waterproof-nylon ground sheet, which can be fashioned as a roof against the elements. In that fashion it won't provide the insulation of a bivy, but it will keep you dry.

Oh yes—food. Run into problems on the trail and survival thinking immediately transforms clothing into shelter, and food into fuel. Keep this in mind when tossing in your snacks at the last minute.

READING TOPOGRAPHIC MAPS

"Unloaded" touring requires that one has a good idea of how much ground can be covered in a day. Paying attention to your day-ride mileages is one, and only one, part of the necessary equation. Next comes a recent and hopefully accurate weather report, for while rain makes paved roads slick, it transforms dirt roads into muck. A third bit of needed information is trail/road condition, at least as much as is possible to gain. And fourth—a *giant* factor in how far you'll ride—is terrain.

There are two kinds of maps—flat, and topographic (most often referred to as "topos"). Flat maps tell you the distance between two points; topos let you know how much up and down there is in between.

This elevation gain or loss is indicated through the use of "contour lines." The theory is simple, and in half an hour a neophyte can be reading topos like a pro. At the bottom of each map is a "contour interval" designation of so many feet. Large-scale, single-state maps (1:500,000 scale; one inch equals eight miles) have an interval of five hundred feet. That is, every time a contour line is encountered along your route you will be gaining or losing five hundred feet of elevation (occasional figures on these lines tell you whether that's up- or downhill). If your path is free of these lines, you're pedaling the plains (or struggling up and zooming down a lot of 499-foot hills that don't show up). If half a dozen of these lines exist in close proximity, you know you're pulling a mountain pass.

The next scale of topos I sometimes use to get an overall feel for a region I'm touring is 1:250,000; one inch equals four miles, contour interval is two hundred feet. These are obviously far more detailed, but still insufficient for the exacting needs of mountain bikers. After all, a series of steep one-hundred-foot climbs can have you panting in an hour; a day of them will see your reservation given to a motorist (heaven forbid), or a cyclist whose more detailed topos allowed a timely arrival.

Better by far for those on ATBs is the 1:62,500 scale; one inch equals one mile, contour level of eighty feet. But best of all is the 1:24,000 scale (known as "7.5 minute," pronounced as seven-and-a-half minute); one inch equals two thousand feet, contour interval most often of forty feet. The detail on these last

Topo map with 1:500,000 scale.
1" = 8 miles
Contour interval 500'

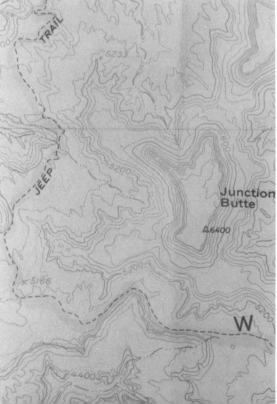

Topo map with 1:62,500 scale.
1" = 1 mile
Contour level 80'

maps is amazing, and with the addition of a "planimeter" (accent on the second syllable) you will have an excellent idea of what lies ahead. (Sometimes called simply a "map measurer," the planimeter has a tiny metal wheel that you roll along the map; a needle and gauge compute the inches traveled, and you multiply this by whatever scale map you're using. This gives you your distance, the contour lines provide the elevation gain and loss.)

Topographic maps also provide detailed road classifications. Different colorings or markings indicate the categories of interstate, heavy-duty, medium-duty, light-duty, unimproved dirt roads and jeep trails. Map symbols include everything from footbridges and overpasses to dams and canals. Various shadings indicate swamps, wooded marshes, vineyards, orchards, and more. If your route takes you past a glacier, your topo will show you the best way around it.

But this detail comes at a cost—that of so many maps being required for relatively short rides. For example, I recently completed a tough 107-mile ride along the Lolo Trail, following Lewis and Clark's (and the 1877 Nez Perce retreat) route across Idaho's Bitterroot Mountains. I needed thirteen 7.5-minute maps to cover the distance, and supplemented them with one excellent Forest Service map to provide a single-glance view of the route, as well as other kinds of information like campgrounds and ranger stations.

Not wishing to ruin my topos on the trail, I photocopied them and left the originals at home. Some copy centers have machines large enough to handle an entire 7.5 minute map, but I prefer to use a regular (less expensive) machine, set on 11″ × 17″ size, and copy only that portion of the map covering my trail. To avoid confusion I number these copies sequentially. Before the trip I use a colorful "hi-liter" to high-light my intended route, but not obscure it. When on the trail I sometimes note locations of certain sites (especially when following historic routes) on my copies. But if not they serve perfectly for starting campfires.

6

The ATB Controversy: Trail Etiquette and Wilderness Prohibition

THIS IS SURELY the most explosive issue in mountain biking. Let's begin with some facts.

1. In 1964, in an attempt to "establish a National Wilderness Preservation system for the permanent good of the whole people," the U.S. Congress passed the Wilderness Act. Designated lands were to be set aside, to remain *natural*— pure, pristine, and untrammeled.

To guard against the erosion of this natural condition, Section 4(c) of the Act stated:

> . . . there shall be no temporary road, no use of motor vehicles, motorized equipment or motor boats, no landing aircraft, no other form of mechanical transport, and no structure . . . within such area.

2. Today, a quarter-century later, Section 4(c) of the Wilderness Act remains unchanged.

3. In 1964 mountain bikes had not been born.

4. Mountain bikes are not motorized. They are, however, a "form of mechanical transport," and as such are excluded. For a time there was confusion on this issue, primarily as a result of the Forest Service regulations set forth in 1965 concerning how the Wilderness Act provisions would be implemented for

those lands under Department of Agriculture jurisdiction. (Got that?) The Forest Service, in the Code of Federal Regulations (CFR) section 293.6(a), defined "mechanical transport" as:

> . . . any contrivance which travels over ground . . .on wheels . . . and is propelled by a non-living power source . . . contained or carried . . . on the device.

Some mountain bikers therefore believed their vehicles were allowed in wilderness areas. But in 1983 Forest Service Chief Max Peterson did away with this confusion by stating the Wilderness Act regulatory language was applicable to *all* wildernesses. In effect, mountain bike use in any wilderness area was, and remains, prohibited.

5.   Some cyclists still hope for a revision of the Wilderness Act prohibition, arguing that if ATBs had been present in 1964 their use would have been allowed. Ed Bloedel, of the U.S. Forest Service in Washington, D.C., is perhaps representative of the opposite position:

> It's the cumulative effect of things like this that really hurt our national wilderness system. Once you begin making little exceptions here and there you begin to lose what you're trying to provide in the first place—a chunk of primitive America, of something that is essentially the same as our forefathers found it.

Beyond this point, it took eight years of wrangling for Congress to pass the Wilderness Act, and any change to allow the use of mountain bikes would bring about a firestorm of protest and intense lobbying efforts by individuals and environmental organizations. Says Sally Reid, Sierra Club officer, "If you think bicycles can get into the Wilderness Act you just don't know how the United States feels about it, about that Act. Nobody is going to monkey with that. There would be an uproar if anyone tried to open up wilderness areas to vehicles."

6.   The use of ATBs is not permitted in:
   a) *wilderness areas*
   b) *national parks*   (except on roads, and those paths specifically marked "bike path")
   c) *national monuments* (except on roads open to the public)
   d) *most state parks and monuments* (except on roads, and those paths specifically marked "bike path")
   e) an increasing number of *urban and county parks*, especially in California (except on roads, and those paths specifically marked "bike path")

The Wilderness Act keeps thousands of trails off-limits to mountain bikes.

7. The use of ATBs is at present allowed on *national forest* roads and trails, except for those in wilderness or primitive areas, and on those trails marked with signs declaring "no bikes allowed," or declared off-limits to bikes on the appropriate "travel map." (Travel maps showing permissible vehicular use are available from national forest local district offices.)

8. Of the approximately 100,000 miles of trails in national forests, roughly 32,000 are in wilderness areas.

9. The use of ATBs is at present allowed on Bureau of Land Management (BLM) lands. BLM administers 334 million acres nationally. Some of the regions have seasonal limited-use restrictions, due to possible animal disturbance. And some have signs requiring road travel only, due to fragile ecosystems.

10. The Sierra Club, as one of many environmental organizations opposed to mountain bike use in wilderness areas and on some other lands, amended their previous (and similar) position by adopting the following "Policy on Off-Road Use of Vehicles" in May '88:

> The Sierra Club reaffirms its support for the Wilderness Act's prohibition of "mechanized modes of transport," including non-motorized vehicles, from entry into designated wilderness.

> Concerning "Use of vehicles on other public lands":

> Trails and areas on public lands should be closed to all vehicles unless (1) determined to be appropriate for their use through completion of an analysis, review, and implementation process, and (2) officially posted with signs as being open.

> The process must include (1) application of objective criteria to assess whether or not environmental quality can be effectively maintained, and whether the safety and enjoyment of all users can be protected; (2) a public review and comment procedure involving all interested parties; and (3) promulgation of effective implementing regulations where impacts are sufficiently low that vehicle use is appropriate.

> Trails and areas designated for vehicular use must be monitored periodically to detect environmental damage or user interference inconsistent with the above criteria. Where this occurs, the trail or area must be closed to vehicles unless effective corrective regulations are enforced.

11. The topics of "environmental damage" and "user interference" are continuing sources of disagreement. Many mountain bikers contend that the few trail-impact studies which have been done indicate their impact is far less

damaging than that of horses, and that it is the very few "kamikaze" riders who tear up the soil, frighten animals, and bother fellow trail-users who give all mountain bikers a bad name.

12.   In an attempt to defuse the conflict between cyclists and hiker/equestrians (and thereby deter further trail closings to mountain bikes), many national off-road bicycle organizations have formed, and are providing guidelines to their members for safe, responsible trail use. One of the largest of these—NORBA (National Off-Road Bicycle Association)—publishes the following code of behavior:

   1.   I will yield the right of way to other non-motorized recreationists. I realize that people judge all cyclists by my actions.
   2.   I will slow down and use caution when approaching or overtaking another and will make my presence known well in advance.
   3.   I will maintain control of my speed at all times and will approach turns in anticipation of someone around the bend.
   4.   I will stay on designated trails to avoid trampling native vegetation and minimize potential erosion to trails by not using muddy trails or short-cutting switchbacks.
   5.   I will not disturb wildlife or livestock.
   6.   I will not litter. I will pack out what I pack in, and pack out more than my share whenever possible.
   7.   I will respect public and private property, including trail use signs, no trespassing signs, and I will leave gates as I have found them.
   8.   I will always be self-sufficient and my destination and travel speed will be determined by my ability, my equipment, the terrain, the present and potential weather conditions.
   9.   I will not travel solo when bikepacking in remote areas. I will leave word of my destination and when I plan to return.
   10.   I will observe the practice of minimum impact bicycling by "taking only pictures and memories and leaving only waffle prints."
   11.   I will always wear a helmet whenever I ride.

13.   Some national forests are establishing "guidelines" for mountain bikers, as in the following sheet distributed to riders by Utah's Wasatch-Cache National Forest office. It's an excellent "code of ethics" for bikers:

Study a Forest Map Before You Ride
Currently, bicycles are permitted on roads and developed trails within the Wasatch-Cache National Forest except in designated Wilderness. If your route crosses private land, it is your responsibility to obtain right of way permission from the land owner.

Keep Groups Small
Riding in large groups degrades the outdoor experience for others, can disturb wildlife and usually leads to greater resource damage.

Avoid Riding on Wet Trails
Bicycle tires leave ruts in wet trails. These ruts concentrate runoff and accelerate erosion. Postponing a ride when the trails are wet will preserve the trails for future use.

Stay on Roads and Trails
Riding cross-country destroys vegetation and damages the soil.

Always Yield to Others
Trails are shared by hikers, horses and bicycles. Move off the trail to allow horses to pass and stop to allow hikers adequate room to share the trail. Simply yelling "bicycle" is not acceptable.

Control Your Speed
Excessive speed endangers yourself and other forest users.

Avoid Wheel Lock-up and Spin-out
Steep terrain is especially vulnerable to trail wear. Locking brakes on steep descents, or when stopping, needlessly damages trails. If a slope is steep enough to require locking wheels and skidding, dismount and walk your bicycle. Likewise, if an ascent is so steep your rear wheel slips and spins, dismount and walk your bicycle.

Protect Waterbars and Switchbacks
Waterbars, the rock and log drains built to direct water off trails, protect trails from erosion. When you encounter a waterbar, ride directly over the top or dismount and walk your bicycle. Riding around the ends of waterbars destroys them and speeds erosion. Skidding around switchback corners shortens trail life. Slow for switchback corners and keep your wheels rolling.

If You Abuse It—You Lose It
Mountain bikes are relative newcomers to the forest and must prove themselves responsible trail users. By following the guidelines above, and by participating in trail maintenance service projects, bicyclists can help avoid closures which would prevent them from using trails.

So much for the relevant facts. The arguments and issues surrounding the ATB-in-wilderness controversy are many and varied, sometimes (as the saying goes) generating more heat than light. One thing is certain. *Most* mountain bikers want to enjoy the same pristine wilderness championed by conservationists. The exceptions are the "banzai" or "kamikaze" riders, out there for the thrill and danger of it all, who could use a few good lessons in both courtesy and environmental science. For the rest of us, we face the task of deciding for ourselves if, where, when, and how the wilderness should be opened to mountain bikes.

Opinions vary widely. NORBA Director Chris Ross stresses the fact that most of his members are following NORBA's eleven-point code and that a few "bad apples" are distorting the bikers' image: "For every two hundred people who follow the code, it only takes one or two banzai guys to ruin things. No one notices all the rest who do no damage; they only notice those who do it wrong."

Sierra Club officer Sally Reid takes a similar tack for non-Wilderness trails: "Trails must be analyzed by land managers for their appropriateness for bicycle use. . . . Obviously there are trails which should be left open to [mountain bikers]; I have no objection to bicycles on trails where I can see them, and where they can see me." But on the issue of opening federally-designated Wilderness areas to mountain bikers, Reid is unequivocal: "No. It's too disturbing to animals. It's too disturbing to people. It's too disturbing to vegetation. Just no!"

There are as many positions on the issue as there are people willing to voice an opinion. For my thoughts on the matter, I accept the validity of many parts of the arguments put forth by those who wish a change in the Wilderness Act. I also see the inherent difficulties in the Sierra Club proposal that public land trails be excluded until open to bikes, rather than the reverse (which is true at present). I admit also that recent studies indicate that horse traffic is in many ways more damaging to trails than are mountain bikes. And, of course, it is obvious that noisy, rowdy hikers and/or equestrians are more disturbing to fellow trail users and animals than the occasional quiet cyclist.

I know these things from my many conversations with fellow cyclists around the nation, and with the many forest service and park service personnel I meet during my annual two-wheeled travels. And you should know, from my earlier comments in this book, that the continued exclusion of wilderness lands from mountain bikers forces me to don something I hoped to give up long ago—a backpack. After all, I wish to see more of these wilderness regions than those few miles I can reach on a day hike. And I don't own a horse.

Nevertheless, I must continue to support our wilderness exclusion. My reasons are primarily not environmental, given my agreement that most mountain bikers are concerned about damage, and that "tender" soils—at least in the harder-to-reach wilderness regions—attract few bikers anyway. No, it is almost exclusively for aesthetic reasons that I wish to see our banishment continued. No matter the arguments of how mechanical modern packs or skis or high-tech stoves may be, or how unappealing it is to follow a trail recently traveled by a pack train, horses—and humans with backpacks—do not for me detract from the natural experience that I believe wilderness areas must protect.

Mountain bikes can bring us to remote, beautiful places . . .

I have written before on this subject:

> In this day of man's increasingly mechanical approach to the outdoors,
> when thousands experience nature not for what it is through observa-
> tion but as a playground, there aren't many places left where one is
> guaranteed one won't be run over by a jeep or snowmobile or moun-
> tain bike. Preserving those areas—at the cost of a disgruntled few—
> seems worth the price.

. . . but at what price to the environment?

My feelings, many years and hundreds of conversations later, remain the same. Preservation—of the entire aesthetic experience of wilderness for Man, and not simply environmental purity—is for me what it's all about. Even if a perfectly quiet, non-damaging ATB were invented, I would not want it whizzing by me in the wilderness. Because, for a moment, I would be mentally transported to the urban vehicular world which I had traveled here to escape.

I support as well the Sierra Club policy of "trail studies first, *then* official openings." Why? Because, simply, of the chance to do too much damage to some environmentally sensitive trails, and more especially to fellow trail users on the busier, near-urban routes. My forest service friends contend they have enough to do as it is, but I believe it would not be impossible, in say a year to eighteen months, to determine the status of at least our most-used trails.

We may be forced off our favorite single tracks for a season during the assessment process, and made to satisfy ourselves with jeep roads and other routes. For that matter, we may lose access to a few of our favorite trails forever, especially if they are close to towns and thus put us in conflict with fellow users (as has happened recently in Boulder, Colorado). But I honestly believe this process would mean the preservation and *permanent* opening of far more trail miles to us in the future.

7

Maintenance and Repair

I F YOU ARE like most normal people you *hate* the idea of working on your bike, and will not consult this chapter until it's absolutely necessary. That is, until your failure to pick up the many maintenance tips sprinkled throughout the following pages, and your consequent inability to learn the machine beneath you and keep it lubed and finely tuned with very little effort, insures the need for major repair. Too bad.

Mountain bike manufacturers, knowing how their rigs are beaten about and generally mistreated, have produced amazingly durable bikes which consequently require little effort to keep in good working order. Almost everything is obvious on a mountain bike: most components can be removed with a simple allen (or hex) wrench; wheels are wider and shorter than those found on spindly thin-tire bikes, requiring far less care no matter the trail bashing they take; little on a beefy ATB is so delicate that it will break if handled somewhat incorrectly when you first attempt repair. And even those things that are more difficult to reach—the sealed bearings hiding away in pedals, wheel hubs, headsets and bottom brackets—make life much easier for everyone. I'll show you how to reach those bearings for the infrequent times when they require service. But, because they are sealed, you will go a very long time between cleanings.

In short, you don't have to be a mechanic to maintain a mountain bike, or to follow the simple instructions in this chapter. If you, like me, have not been blessed with mechanical aptitude, or if you do possess such a mind but simply haven't yet been schooled in which end of a wrench does the work, much of the following at first glance will appear impossible to master. But then so did learning to tie your shoes.

So take it easy, *slowly*. Read the procedures with the bike before you, for otherwise you'll be lost. Remember that it's all mechanical, that you can *see* what's happening when you turn a screw or tighten a spoke. We're not splitting atoms here, nor following electrons through some difficult circuitry on a computer chip. So don't give up at the first hint of confusion. And if at some point you do have to wheel your rig to the bike shop for expert care, ask the man or woman in the mechanic's apron if you can watch.

TOOLS

As mentioned in earlier chapters, most commuters and trail riders out for a day pack only a set of allen wrenches, six-inch crescent, small screwdriver, tire levers, air pump and a spare tube (and/or patch kit). The following list, however, and the accompanying drawing, include both my on-the-road and at-home tools.

1. *Crescent wrench—15":* I far prefer a vise to pull my freewheel, but this does a good job of it and is far less expensive. When at home I use it in place of my "pocket vise," and also instead of my six-inch crescent for pulling off a cotterless crank (the six-inch must be used when on the road, but the strain on this small tool is great).

2. *Crescent wrench—6":* The most-used tool by cyclists. Be sure to buy quality, for the slide mechanism on a cheap one will in time refuse to stay cinched tightly against a nut.

3. *Crescent wrench—4":* Very nice for brake work, if you don't plan to purchase a set of metric open or box ends. Remember that this tool, like so many others pictured, will not be carried on the road and isn't really necessary for home repair. It's included simply because it makes some jobs easier than do the larger wrenches.

4. *Channel locks—7":* This is an excellent road tool for tightening headsets, and for gripping anything too large for the six-inch crescent. It is part of my personal commuting/day-riding/touring kit.

5. *Vise grips:* A larger pair is required to remove blips from rim walls, something you may never need to do if you're lucky and keep your tires properly inflated.

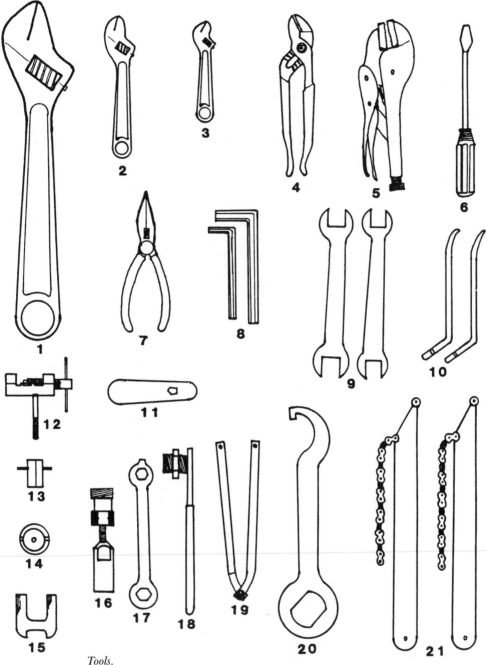

Tools.

1) crescent wrench—15"
2) crescent wrench—6"
3) crescent wrench—4"
4) channel locks—7"
5) vise grips
6) regular blade screwdriver
7) needle-nose pliers
8) allen wrenches
9) cone wrenches
10) tire levers
11) Swiss Army Knife
12) chain rivet tool
13) spoke nipple wrench
14) freewheel tool
15) pocket vise
16) cotterless crank removal tool
17) universal cotterless crank wrench
18) universal cotterless crankarm puller
19) universal adjustable cup tool
20) lock ring/fixed cup bottom bracket tool
21) freewheel sprocket tools

6. *Regular blade screwdriver:* I pack a thin, lightweight, short-handled screwdriver which, with long shank included, measures six inches in length; the flat blade tip (only ³⁄₁₆″ wide) is perfect for very fine adjustments of derailleur set screws. Buy a poor quality screwdriver and the blade will bend and chip in no time.

7. *Needle-nose pliers:* I prefer a small pair with side-cutters (for trimming brake and gear cables).

8. *Allen (hex) wrenches:* Do not leave on a long ride without making sure you have an allen wrench for each and every size allen head on the bike, for the Fates will surely cause that single bolt you've overlooked to loosen up. Also, do not try to get by with an allen wrench which "almost" fits; you'll end up rounding off the corners and ruining the bolt.

9. *Cone wrenches:* Make sure they are thin, lightweight, and that they fit your cones. The far heavier shop models are best left at home.

10. *Tire levers:* I pack only two, for I find the third one sold in most sets to be unnecessary. The tips must be perfectly smooth, or you'll be puncturing your tube while trying to repair it.

11. *Swiss Army knife:* Extremely handy for many reasons (including an extremely thin blade for removing seals). I carry one, primarily on very long rides.

12. *Chain rivet tool:* Necessary for removing a chain, adding links, and freeing frozen links. Be sure the rivet tool you're buying will fit the chain on your bike.

13. *Spoke nipple wrench:* The "T" type is pictured; this model, and the "hoop" style wrench, are my preferences over the round multi-size nipple wrenches. Make sure the wrench you purchase will fit your spokes.

14. *Freewheel tool:* Most freewheels require removal tools specific to their brand. Match these up before hitting the road, for removal of the freewheel is necessary for spoke replacement on the freewheel side (a *very* infrequent repair). Most cassette-type freewheels require a freewheel cog removal tool for spoke replacement.

15. *Pocket vise:* These wonderful creations are necessary—along with the freewheel tool above—for most freewheel removals on the road. Large vises, or the fifteen-inch crescent wrench mentioned, are my preferences at home, but this little beauty would have made life much easier on my round-the-world ride.

16. *Cotterless crank removal tool:* Again, make sure it fits your bike. I carry this with me always.

17. *Universal cotterless crank wrench:* For use with the following item; home tool only, and only if you work on several cranks of different sizes.

18. *Universal cotterless crankarm puller:* The previous tool removes the "crankarm fixing bolt" (that wonderful advance of technology beyond the formerly ubiquitous cotter pins); this tool pulls the crankarm to allow access to the bottom bracket hub.

19. *Universal adjustable cup tool:* This is excellent for home use, but far too heavy for the road. Only on my longest tours do I work on my bottom bracket, and then I use a screwdriver blade tip to adjust the bottom bracket bearing pressure.

20. *Lock ring/fixed cup bottom bracket tool:* For adjustments of the bottom bracket lock ring and fixed cup; home use only.

21. *Freewheel sprocket tools:* Home use. If you have a large vise you'll need only one; two are otherwise required to change sprockets. Most people toss their entire freewheels when only a couple of cogs need replacement (the smallest two, usually)—a far less expensive repair than buying all new sprockets plus the center "core" body filled with ball bearings.

22. *Sealed bearing tools/roller cam brake tool* (not pictured): Most mountain bikes have "sealed" bearings in one or more areas—pedals, headset, hubs, bottom bracket. Many of these seals can be removed easily with one or more of the tools above, or very carefully with a thin knife blade, but some are more conveniently removed with specific tools for this purpose. Your dealer will point out these seals to you (and the purpose of the roller cam brake tool) and will either have the appropriate tool for sale or can order it. Don't be afraid to ask that he show you how to use these, but be prepared to return to the shop at some time convenient to *him* for the instruction. (If your schedule allows it, try to hit bike shops at times other than Friday afternoons and Saturdays.)

Beyond the tools listed above, tune-up stands of many kinds are available, plus wheel truing stands which make that job far easier. Finally, a floor pump with built-in gauge and flip-off air nozzle is a must if you ride daily.

SADDLE

A good bike shop will help you determine general saddle position when sizing you for your bike, but most riders find slight adjustments of height, tilt, and position toward or away from the handlebars necessary to produce that perfect fit of cycle and cyclist. The quick-release (q-r) lever will allow extremely fast

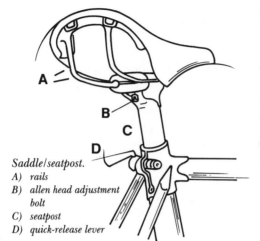

Saddle/seatpost.
A) rails
B) allen head adjustment
   bolt
C) seatpost
D) quick-release lever

Under-the-saddle allen head adjustment bolt
(for changing tilt and fore/aft position of
saddle).

changes in saddle height, and most mountain bike seat posts require only an
allen wrench to alter tilt and forward/aft position.

Height —This is a rough one, so pay close attention. First, flip the q-r
lever. Second, adjust the saddle height. Third, close the q-r lever tightly.

Tilt —Saddle tilt is a very individual preference. I suggest you begin with
no slant whatsoever, and work from there. You need merely loosen the be-
neath-the-saddle allen fittings, position the saddle as desired, and tighten.

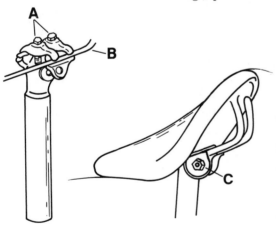

*Quick-release seat post lever;
notice graduated seat post.*

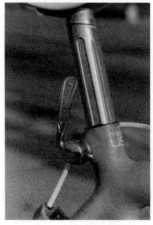

Saddle/seatpost #2
A) adjustment bolts
B) rail
C) old-style clamp and belt

Forward/backward movement —You'll recall I mentioned this in the earlier discussion of bike fit. The saddle has the ability to move toward or away from the handlebars along its "rails" (look beneath the saddle for these). This distance, plus top tube and handlebar stem length, allow an extremely personal fit. Pay attention to slight arm, neck, and lower back strain if you are too far or too close to the bars, and adjust accordingly. Remember that a good bike shop will provide a general fit, but you must tailor it precisely to your own body and riding style. Again, simply loosen the allen bolt or bolts beneath the saddle, slide the saddle along its rails, and tighten again.

Side-to-side movement —The saddle nose should of course point directly over the top tube. If it has worked itself off-center, flip the quick-release seat post bolt, position correctly, then close tightly.

HANDLEBAR/HEADSET

Don't be scared by all the parts of a headset, for chances are excellent, especially with an ATB's sealed (or "shielded" bearings), that you'll never have to deal with them when out on the road or trail. Most riders *never* work on their headsets, except when erroneously thinking it necessary to raise or lower the handlebars. The following words are provided, therefore, to help you understand this usually neglected portion of your bike, and to facilitate adjustments and repairs if necessary.

First, the headset's job is not to hold the handlebar in place. (This is done by the bar's own expander bolt/wedge assembly, as you'll soon see.) Its purpose, instead, is to secure the fork to the frame in such a manner as to allow free rotation to the right and left. Now look closely at the drawing and you'll see how this is performed. The top of the fork is threaded, and is held in place in

Headset.

A) *locknut*
B) *lock washer*
C) *adjusting cup/top threaded race*
D) *bearings*

E) *top head/set race*
F) *head tube*
G) *bottom head/set race*
H) *fork crown race*
I) *fork*

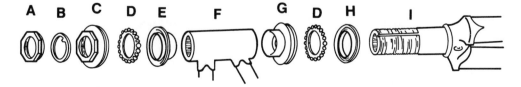

A B C D E F G D H I

the head tube by the top threaded race (bearing cup). This race, and the fork crown race, are positioned with the top and bottom bearings to allow for rotation. In all my riding the greatest difficulty I've had with headsets (a slight difficulty in turning the bars side-to-side) was remedied in the following fifteen-minute repair.

First, using my large crescent when at home, or the channel locks on the road, I loosen the large lock nut at the top of the headset. Next, I loosen the top threaded race, but only slightly, until I can see the bearings inside but *before* they can escape (something which won't happen if you have the ball retainer rings common to many bikes today, and especially if they are sealed). I then squirt cycle oil into the mass of bearings, very carefully allow the fork to slip down a fraction of an inch to expose the bottom bearings, and add oil there. This done I tighten the top threaded race, then the lock nut on top, until there is no upward or downward movement within the headset, but free movement of the fork side to side.

Bar height adjustment —Notice the expander bolt in the drawing. At the other end of this bolt—inside the head tube—is either an angled expander nut or a wedge nut (an "exterior" or "interior" wedge). When the expander bolt is tightened the angled nut presses against the head tube wall; the wedge nut type works by drawing the nut up inside the stem, forcing the stem walls out against the head tube.

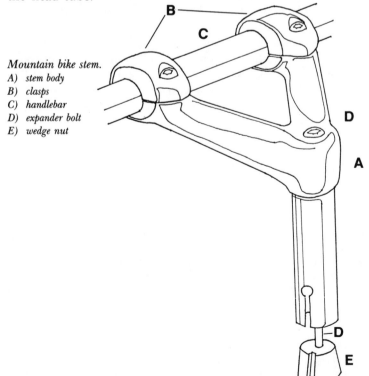

Mountain bike stem.
A) *stem body*
B) *clasps*
C) *handlebar*
D) *expander bolt*
E) *wedge nut*

Now take the second important step in all mechanical repairs: a *close* look at everything which might be affected or at all involved. In the case of lowering or raising bars, many brake assemblies are involved (through the lengthening or shortening of the brake cable). If this is so with your bars, simply disengage the brake cable until the bar is adjusted, then readjust cable length.

Loosen the expander bolt. Don't be concerned if the wedge nut comes off the expander bolt, for it can't fall far. Just turn the bike upside down and the nut will come free. If your bike is brand new, your bars can be moved when the expander bolt is loosened, but if not, you'll have to re-thread the expander bolt a couple turns into the frozen angled or wedge nut inside the head tube, and then rap it lightly with a mallet (or something similar). Position the bars as desired—being *sure* to leave at least two full inches of stem inside the head tube (critical on a mountain bike, due to the tremendous beating the handlebars take)—and tighten the expander bolt.

Bars off-center —Sometimes a fall will cause one's bars not to point straight over the wheel. In this case simply loosen the expander bolt assembly (as above), re-position, and tighten securely.

Loose brake lever —On a mountain bike the allen head fitting is easy to see; re-position and tighten.

BRAKES

A thorough study of these assemblies will go far in reducing any fears in working on them. You will see a cable leading from the brake handle, through a cable adjustment system of some kind, to the wheel brake component. When the hand brake is squeezed the cable length is shortened, pulling the brake pads toward the wheel rim until contact is made. Simple.

Difficulties are encountered when, after much use, the brake pads have worn down, or the cable has stretched, become slightly rusted inside its housing, or broken. The first two problems are remedied with no tools at all, and can in fact be accomplished from the saddle.

Worn pads and cable stretch —Look back to your cable adjustment assembly—where an "adjustment barrel" of one shape or another shortens the cable when turned counterclockwise; a locknut or lock ring beneath the barrel must be loosened to allow adjustment, then tightened again to hold the barrel in place.

After many miles a cable might require more adjustment than that possible through these assemblies. In this case, begin by screwing down the barrel completely (to allow for greater adjustments later), then loosen the "cable anchor bolt" (it will be obvious which bolt and nut combination hold the cable in

Installation of the cantilever brake

2 ■ **Installation of the wire**

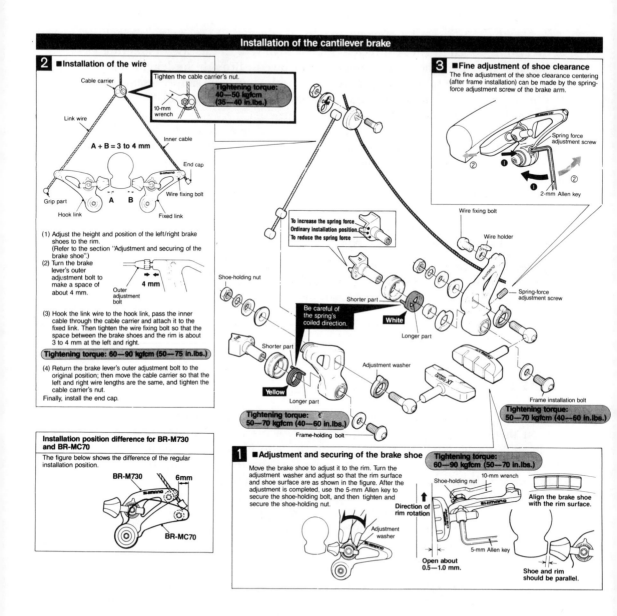

Cable carrier

Tighten the cable carrier's nut.

Tightening torque: 40—50 kgfcm (35—40 in.lbs.)

10-mm wrench

Link wire

A + B = 3 to 4 mm

Inner cable

End cap

Grip part

A B

Wire fixing bolt

Hook link

Fixed link

(1) Adjust the height and position of the left/right brake shoes to the rim.
(Refer to the section "Adjustment and securing of the brake shoe".)
(2) Turn the brake lever's outer adjustment bolt to make a space of about 4 mm.

4 mm

Outer adjustment bolt

(3) Hook the link wire to the hook link, pass the inner cable through the cable carrier and attach it to the fixed link. Then tighten the wire fixing bolt so that the space between the brake shoes and the rim is about 3 to 4 mm at the left and right.

Tightening torque: 60—90 kgfcm (50—75 in.lbs.)

(4) Return the brake lever's outer adjustment bolt to the original position; then move the cable carrier so that the left and right wire lengths are the same, and tighten the cable carrier's nut.
Finally, install the end cap.

3 ■ **Fine adjustment of shoe clearance**
The fine adjustment of the shoe clearance centering (after frame installation) can be made by the spring-force adjustment screw of the brake arm.

Spring force adjustment screw

2-mm Allen key

Wire fixing bolt

Wire holder

Spring-force adjustment screw

To increase the spring force
Ordinary installation position
To reduce the spring force

Shoe-holding nut

Shorter part

White

Longer part

Be careful of the spring's coiled direction.

Shorter part

Adjustment washer

Yellow

Longer part

Tightening torque: 50—70 kgfcm (40—60 in.lbs.)

Frame-holding bolt

Frame installation bolt

Tightening torque: 50—70 kgfcm (40—60 in.lbs.)

Installation position difference for BR-M730 and BR-MC70
The figure below shows the difference of the regular installation position.

BR-M730   6mm

BR-MC70

1 ■ **Adjustment and securing of the brake shoe**
Move the brake shoe to adjust it to the rim. Turn the adjustment washer and adjust so that the rim surface and shoe surface are as shown in the figure. After the adjustment is completed, use the 5-mm Allen key to secure the shoe-holding bolt, and then tighten and secure the shoe-holding nut.

Tightening torque: 60—90 kgfcm (50—70 in.lbs.)

10-mm wrench

Shoe-holding nut

Direction of rim rotation

Adjustment washer

Open about 0.5—1.0 mm.

5-mm Allen key

Align the brake shoe with the rim surface.

Shoe and rim should be parallel.

These detailed drawings and instructions (courtesy of Shimano) will help you adjust and/or repair your bike no matter its brand of componentry. Again, go slowly and logically from step to step.

place, as the cable passes directly through it). Ideally, this should be done with the brake pads pressed against the rim, so as to estimate proper cable position. A "third-hand tool" may be used for this purpose, or a fellow rider. But far more often I simply squeeze the pads together, toward the rim, then lift free one end of the short transverse cable (also called "center wire")—the cable running from the top of either brake arm, at the end of the long brake cable stretching from the brake handle to the brake assembly on the wheel. Normally this technique is used to allow for the fast removal of tires, as this moves the brake pads away from the rim sufficiently to allow the larger tire profile to pass. But when adjusting brakes I do it so as to loosen the cable anchor bolt, take up a slight amount of slack cable, tighten the cable anchor bolt again and re-set the brake. It's seldom perfectly correct the first time around, but very close on the second.

Brake pads, by the way, should be set close enough to the rim to insure the fast, strong application of brake pad force against the rim with only the slightest movement of the brake handle. With poorly adjusted brakes a precious second is lost while cable slack is taken up through the hard squeezing of the brake handle. Not only can this delay in reaction time be costly, but the pressure of pad against rim will be reduced. Naturally, a well-aligned wheel is necessary if pads are to be mounted close to the rim.

Rubber brake pads once came mounted in their metal "shoes" in such a way that replacement pads were easily installed. The shoes had one end open— that end, of course, which must be mounted *against* the direction of wheel rotation (open end toward the back of the bike). Otherwise the pads would merely shoot forward out of their shoes, leaving you to white-knuckle your way to a thrilling, unassisted stop. Most shoe/pad arrangements today are a single piece, which unfortunately requires a more costly—if idiot-proof—replacement. Just be thoughtful during the replacement if you have the older style.

Adjustment of the Shimano U-brake is explained by that company's artwork; the SunTour roller cam cable or brake arm tension is adjusted easily with the roller cam brake tool (available through dealers) holding the brake arms (and thus the pads) in place.

Cable replacement/lubrication —Watch carefully as you remove the broken cable from its housing and you'll learn almost all you need to know for replacement. Notice the ball (or pear- or cylinder-shaped) end of the cable, held in place by the brake handle housing. Brake cables come with one end which will fit your particular housing; the other end is to be cut off (carefully, so that the individual metal strands do not fray) to allow its placement into the cable housing, and final entry into the tiny hole in the cable anchor bolt, or far more easily laid into the slotted washer groove. (I use the side-cutter portion of

Installation and adjustment of the U-brake

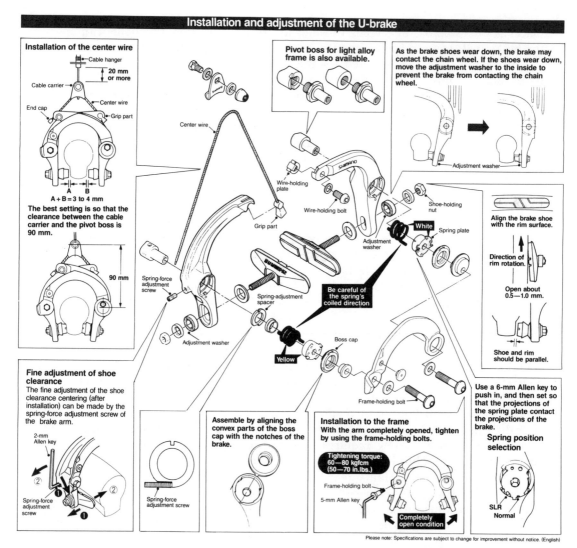

Installation of the center wire

Cable hanger

20 mm or more

Cable carrier

Center wire

End cap

Grip part

A   B

A + B = 3 to 4 mm

The best setting is so that the clearance between the cable carrier and the pivot boss is 90 mm.

90 mm

Fine adjustment of shoe clearance

The fine adjustment of the shoe clearance centering (after installation) can be made by the spring-force adjustment screw of the brake arm.

2-mm Allen key

②

②

Spring-force adjustment screw

Spring-force adjustment screw

Assemble by aligning the convex parts of the boss cap with the notches of the brake.

Center wire

Pivot boss for light alloy frame is also available.

Wire-holding plate

Wire-holding bolt

Grip part

Spring-force adjustment screw

Spring-adjustment spacer

Adjustment washer

Be careful of the spring's coiled direction

Yellow

Adjustment washer

Boss cap

Frame-holding bolt

Installation to the frame

With the arm completely opened, tighten by using the frame-holding bolts.

Tightening torque: 60—80 kgfcm (50—70 in.lbs.)

Frame-holding bolt

5-mm Allen key

Completely open condition

As the brake shoes wear down, the brake may contact the chain wheel. If the shoes wear down, move the adjustment washer to the inside to prevent the brake from contacting the chain wheel.

Adjustment washer

Shoe-holding nut

White   Spring plate

Align the brake shoe with the rim surface.

Direction of rim rotation.

Open about 0.5—1.0 mm.

Shoe and rim should be parallel.

Use a 6-mm Allen key to push in, and then set so that the projections of the spring plate contact the projections of the brake.

Spring position selection

SLR

Normal

Please note: Specifications are subject to change for improvement without notice. (English)

Courtesy Shimano

my needle-nose pliers for this cut when at home, but as I do not carry a needle-nose any longer on the road I have had to resort to more barbaric means. I first crimp the cable strands by placing my screwdriver blade over the cable and tapping the other end with a wrench. Then I work the metal strands back and forth with the channel locks, until they break.)

Once having depressed the brake handle and located the "barrel" end of the broken cable, remove the brake cable. Snip off the unnecessary end of the new cable, lightly grease the cable throughout its length, then insert it beneath the brake handle and into the cable housing. Run its cut end through the cable anchor bolt, and adjust pad placement as discussed above. Excess cable can be wound into a ball or cut off.

Sometimes a slight crack in the cable housing, or a drop of water which manages to find its way inside, will cause brakes to "stick." Although the metal brake arms are usually suspected (a drop or two of oil will keep these working well, and can be applied now to determine if these arms or the cable are at fault), it is more likely that rust has formed inside the housing. Simply release the cable at the cable anchor bolt, slip it completely out of its housing, grease, and reattach. (This will be much easier if the free, cut end of the cable has been kept from fraying by a tiny metal "cable clamp"—a soft metal cup which is slipped over the cable end and secured by a squeeze with the channel locks or needle-nose pliers.)

You must be sure, of course, that when the brakes are depressed the pads strike the rim entirely. This is especially critical with U-brakes, as when misadjusted the pads move up and into the tire (thereby cutting into the tire wall), rather than down and away from the tire and rim as with cantilever brakes.

A final adjustment required with many brakes is the toe-in of brake pads. Look closely at your pads when new and you can see if yours are set in this manner. If they are, you will notice that the portion of the pad closer to the *front* of the bike strikes the rim first (as shown in the U-brake adjustment drawing).

TIRES/SPOKES/WHEEL ALIGNMENT

The wheel consists of many parts: hub assembly, spokes, freewheel in the rear, rim, tape (a cloth, plastic, or rubber strip covering the spoke heads, thus protecting the tube from the spokes), tube, tire, and sometimes tire liner (which I suggest for commuting and cactus-area riding). On-the-road repairs required of these parts are usually caused by flat tires, and wheels out of alignment. Spoke breakage is extremely infrequent, but will be covered simply to put the mind at ease.

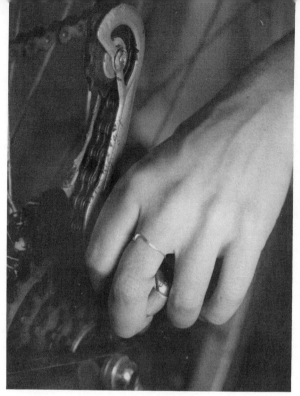

Preparing to lift back the derailleur housing to allow rear wheel removal. (Most flats appear on the rear wheel.)

"Back" position of rear derailleur, to allow rear wheel removal.

Flats —When the cursing is over, assemble the necessary tools: two tire levers, a six-inch crescent (if your wheels aren't quick-release), tube repair kit or spare tube, and air pump.

Remove the wheel. To do so you'll have to put your bike on its back, loosen both axle nuts or trip the quick-release lever, and disengage the short transverse (or center wire) brake cable—to increase the distance between the brake pads sufficiently for the tire to pass between them. (This is the cable running between the top of either brake arm, and to which the main brake cable is attached. Squeeze the pads toward the rim to lift one end of the transverse cable free, as explained in the previous repair procedure.) If it's the front wheel, you can simply lift the wheel out of its dropouts at this point. On the rear wheel, shift the chain into the smallest freewheel sprocket, grab the derailleur body and pull it toward the rear of the bike, and lift the wheel free.

Remove the tire and tube from the rim. This is accomplished with the aid of your tire levers (or spoons). Take the lesser angled end of one spoon and, beveled end up, work it underneath the tire bead about a half-inch. (Begin working with the first lever at a point on the wheel opposite to the valve stem.) Now push down (toward the spokes) on the tire lever in your hand. Hook the slotted side onto a spoke to hold the tire in place (notice drawing). This frees both hands for the rest of the work.

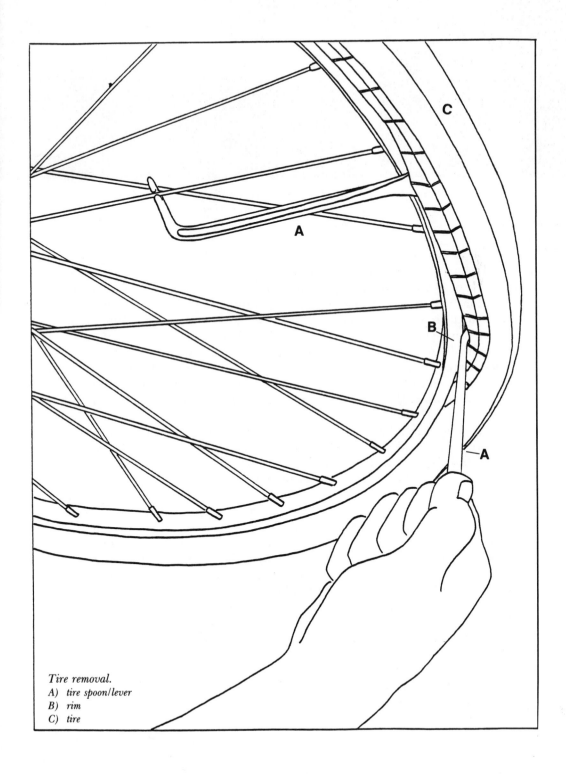

Tire removal.
A) *tire spoon/lever*
B) *rim*
C) *tire*

Closeup of indentation in tire iron; avoid buying tire irons without such indentations

Removal of second bead from tire, freeing tire completely; notice rim tape covering spoke nipple heads.

Tube exposed.

Take a second lever and, once more, work the tip underneath the tire bead, about an inch from the first lever. Again, push down on your lever, to pop the bead away from its seat in the rim. If you can't do this, move your lever a half-inch closer to the first lever. Now continue to work the bead away from the rim all around the wheel, until you have one complete side of the tire free. Then, using your spoon from the opposite side of the wheel, work the second bead off the rim. (You are now working the bead off the rim *away* from you in direction, as of course both beads must come off the same side to free the tire.) Taking one side of the tire off at a time is much easier than trying to force both beads off at once. (Expect a new tire to be more difficult to remove than an old one.)

Remove the tube from the tire, checking both the outside and inside of the tire for embedded glass, thorns, etc. When you're sure that it's clean, move on to the tube. I've had only two holes in my life which leaked so little that I was forced to hold them under water to look for air bubbles. All the other times I merely pumped up the tube and listened for escaping air. (If your tube has a Schrader valve, be sure the air is not escaping from the threaded center valve core. If this core is not screwed tightly into these threads, an air leak will result. The proper tool to tighten a valve core is the "valve cover tool," a tiny slotted metal cap which you should buy to replace the worthless black plastic caps present on all tubes sold. If you have a very slow leak, check that your valve core is tight before you remove the wheel from the frame. I've had this problem only once in twenty years, but it's still worth checking.)

When the hole is located, rough up the area with the patch kit scraper. Be sure to do a good job of it, short of putting additional holes in the tube, and be sure to roughen an area a bit larger than the size of the patch.

Apply the glue, a bit more than necessary to cover the patch area. Most kits suggest waiting until the glue is dry to apply the patch. So, wait. Hurry this step and there's a good chance you'll be taking the wheel off the bike again a few miles down the road. Be careful not to touch the patch side which goes on the tube, and once in place press the edges of the patch with a tire spoon.

When the patch appears to be holding well along the edges, pump a very slight amount of air into the tube to avoid wrinkles when it's placed back inside the tire. Put the tube in the tire, then push the valve stem through the valve stem hole in the rim, and re-seat one of the beads. Once one side of the tire—one bead—is back in place, begin re-seating the second bead. (Removing all air at this point reduces the chance of puncture.) In taking off a tire one begins *opposite* the stem; in replacing it one begins work at the stem and works away from it in both directions, being sure to keep the stem pointing straight up. Riders who fail to do this, or who ride with low air pressure in their tires (which causes the tube to shift and the valve stem to angle out of the hole), cause wearing of the stem along its side and base. Once a hole occurs in the valve stem, the entire tube is shot, for stems can't hold a patch.

You'll probably be able to re-seat all but about six inches of the beads without tools. At this point use your tire spoon in the opposite manner than before—beveled end down.

If both beads are properly seated, and the stem is still perpendicular, inflate the tire to its desired pressure. Do this before you put the wheel back on the bike, for it will mean less to mess with if you've goofed with the patch. But don't worry. A chimp can master a patch kit.

If the tire remains hard for a minute replace the wheel, tighten axle nuts or the quick-release, re-engage the chain if it's the rear wheel, *and* reset your brakes.

Freewheel removal and cleaning —An unfortunate necessity if a rear wheel spoke breaks on the freewheel side (which is almost the *only* place they break, due to the "dishing" discussed in an earlier chapter), today's "pocket vises," and the cassette-type freewheels which can be dismantled with a freewheel cog removal tool, make this repair possible on the road.

Remove the rear wheel, and unscrew and remove the quick-release mechanism. With the Shimano cassette-type freewheel remove the axle, and then

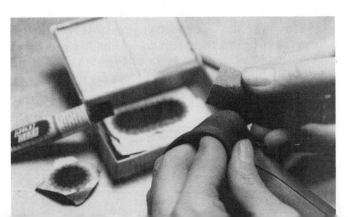

Patch kit showing tube of cement, two patch sizes, tube "rougher" (in hand).

Freewheel removal tool.   *Separating freewheel from rear wheel (where most broken spokes appear).*

unscrew (counterclockwise) the cassette with a ten-millimeter allen wrench. With all others, slide the thin shaft of the quick-release through the pocket vise, freewheel tool (pictured), and freewheel. Center the two prongs of the pocket vise over the handlebar stem, engage the flat sides of the freewheel tool (with the wheel above it), take hold of the wheel at the three and nine o'clock positions and turn counterclockwise. If you're a strong rider, and if the freewheel's not been off the wheel before, you'll have to work at getting it off. Once removed, the spoke heads are visible and replacement can begin.

During those long years before the pocket vise was invented, I struggled with other methods of "breaking" the freewheel. The easiest is finding a regular vise at a home or garage, for the freewheel tool then is set into the vise jaws with its splined or notched teeth pointing up, and the wheel is simply fitted over it and turned (counterclockwise) free. A second relatively easy method is to locate a huge crescent or pipe wrench, place the tire standing up in front of you with freewheel on the right side, engage the freewheel tool into both the freewheel and wrench, and press *downward*.

The hardest of all removals is with the seven-inch channel locks taking the place of a larger wrench, a shock cord wrapped around its handles to hold it together and provide the hand some sort of protection. I've done this only once, when there was no alternative, and it took its toll on both my tool and me. Buy a pocket vise or cassette freewheel.

But what if you haven't a quick-release wheel? I've solved that problem for use with my mountain bike wheels and their large axles by drilling out the

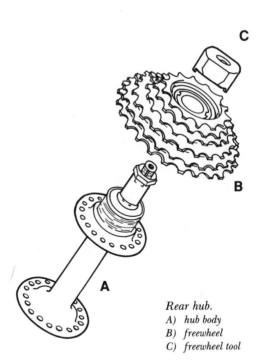

Freewheel tool (top), pocket vise (bottom).

Rear hub.
A) *hub body*
B) *freewheel*
C) *freewheel tool*

tiny hole in the pocket vise sufficiently to accept the axle, and then balancing the wheel and freewheel tool in place over the pocket vise. It's a bit less stable, but it works.

When it comes to cleaning a freewheel, the body (or "core") can be disassembled, but I would do this only if you make watches for a living. My extremely lazy alternative is to set the freewheel upside down (smallest sprocket to the ground) on many sheets of folded newspaper. Now flush the core with Liquid Wrench. This is done by shooting the liquid between the dust ring and main body of the core—just inside the sprocket on the back side. Give the Liquid Wrench a few minutes to work through the bearings. Spin the freewheel several times and move it to a dry piece of paper, then flush again. If the ball bearings inside the core were dirty, the first newspaper will be dark with grease. A third flushing may be necessary. Allow the bearings to dry for a few minutes, then apply a fine, light bicycle oil.

Spoke replacement/wheel alignment —Let's begin with an analysis of the thin, spindly spoke. If you've never thought of it, ponder for a moment how such slender pillars of metal can hold up the weight of a bike, rider, and his gear, while being light enough to spin almost effortlessly in circles around a hub. Now look closely at it; a long shank, threads at the top where it screws into the nipple (protruding through the rim hole and holding the spoke in place and under desired tension), and at the other end a right angle crook which holds it in the hub. That sharp bend is the danger point, the place where when stress becomes too great, life ends. It's curtains for the spoke, curses for the

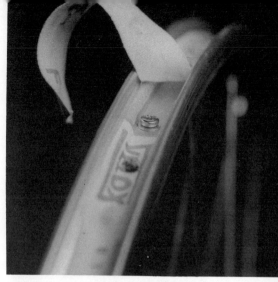

Removing spoke protector plate.   *Rim tape removed, slotted (for screwdriver) spoke nipple shown.*

rider, and an opportunity for the spoke wrench to see daylight once again.

More common, however, is a spoke which simply needs adjustment to help re-align (make "true" again) a wheel. Wheels can be out of true in two ways: they can sway from side to side, and they can have high and low spots, which is referred to as being "out of round." Look closely at your wheel. Notice that the spokes reach out to the rim from both sides of the hub. Focus upon one spoke and think what tightening (shortening the length of) that single spoke will do. The rim will be pulled in two directions at the same time when the spoke is tightened, or moved back in two directions if loosened. Tighten the spoke and the rim will be 1) pulled closer to the hub, and 2) pulled in the direction of the side of the hub to which the other end of the spoke is attached. Loosen the spoke and the opposite movement will occur. Tighten a spoke which comes from the other side of the hub and the rim will move in that direction.

"Truing" a wheel is most quickly and successfully accomplished with the wheel off the bike, the tire, tube, and rim tape removed, and with the assistance of a truing stand. Such stands have small movable metal indicators which one slides ever closer to the rim from both sides as the spoke adjustments bring the wheel increasingly into alignment. This can also be done without a stand, using the bike itself to hold the wheel and one's thumb in place of the metal slides. In fact, since spokes break while riding, and because wheels become untrue generally while I'm touring, I've almost always done this repair while far away from home.

Let's imagine you've broken a spoke on the rear wheel. Begin the repair by flipping your bike on its back, and removing the wheel, tire, tube, and rim tape. If the break is on the freewheel side, remove the freewheel. (If you have a cassette freewheel you may prefer to use freewheel cog removal tools to spin off the first sprocket, disengage the three long metal rods running through the remaining cogs, and then lift off these cogs so as to reach the spoke/hub attach-

Rear-wheel spoking pattern.   *Front wheel spoking pattern.*

ment points.) Put the wheel back on the bike without tightening axle nuts or quick-release. (The spoke can be replaced with the wheel off the bike, but I find it much easier to work with when the wheel is back in place.)

Remove the broken spoke. This is very easy, for spokes break at the bevel, and can then be taken out by pulling from the nipple end.

Take the nipple from the new spoke. Look at the rear hub, and concentrate on the next closest spokes to the one that broke. If you see two spoke heads next to the empty hole in the hub you know that your new spoke must enter from the other side, to follow the alternating pattern around the entire hub. Guide the spoke into the hole. (Don't be afraid to bend the spoke a bit.) Once it is completely through, look at the next closest spoke which enters the hub in the direction as your replacement spoke. This will be your guide on lacing your replacement—how many spokes you must cross, and which to go over or under with the new spoke. (You'll have to bend the spoke even more here; be sure to bend it along its entire length, thereby not putting a crimp in it.)

Put the nipple into the rim, and thread the new spoke into it. Tighten the spoke until it is approximately the same tension as the rest, and then align the wheel (following the procedure below).

I prefer to align wheels with tire, tube, and rim tape removed. This allows for more accurate truing, and exposes the screw head of the spoke nipple for adjustment with a screwdriver (necessary if you've rounded the nipple with the spoke wrench). It also allows you to *see* if too much spoke extends through the nipple head, in which case the metal file blade of the Swiss Army knife can be

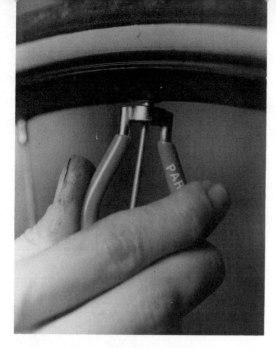

Attachment of new spoke to nipple end after replacement.

used to shorten it. (If you've purchased spare spokes of the proper length you won't be troubled by protrusion.) Restore your freewheel to its proper location, and replace your wheel in the frame (if it isn't already there) as it will be when you ride. Tighten axle nuts or close the quick-release lever, but keep the brakes free.

Standing behind your wheel, with the bike still on its back, spin the wheel with your hand and note the "wobble"—movement side to side.

Determine the extent of the wobble by placing your thumb next to the wheel rim (with the palm of your hand resting on the chainstay), so that your thumbnail lightly touches the rim at every point except for the wobble. At that point the rim will reach out and smack your thumbnail; your job is to pull that wobble back into line with the rest of the rim.

Check the tension of the spokes in the area of the wobble. Chances are they'll be a bit more loose than the rest of the spokes in the wheel. Tighten the spoke at the center of the wobble—just a bit at a time, watching its effect upon the rim—then move on to the spokes on either side. (Read the next two paragraphs before proceeding.)

But how much do you tighten a spoke? And what if two spokes appear to sit right smack in the middle of the problem area? Easy. Just recall that spokes reach out to the rim from both sides of the hub. Naturally, tightening a spoke coming from the right side pulls the rim toward the right; from the left hub side, to the left. If your wobble is to the right, you'll be tightening the spokes which come from the left side of your hub. I always start off with a slight adjustment—about a half-turn for the spoke at wobble center, one-quarter turn for spokes on either side, one-eighth turn for the next two spokes.

On occasion you might have to loosen some spokes and tighten others in the wobble area to produce a true wheel, especially if you have trued your wheel several times before. In loosening spokes, follow the same pattern as above; more toward wobble center, less thereafter.

When your thumbnail-guide tells you all is well, you have two final things to do. First, check your spokes for approximately the same tension on all. You won't be perfect on this, but at least be close or you'll be aligning your wheel again real soon. Second, step to the side of your bike, spin the wheel and check for its "round." If you have one high spot tighten the spokes slightly in this area—to pull the rim toward the hub a bit. But be sure to watch that you don't lose your side-to-side true as you do this.

Let me add that I find wheel alignment to be the most delicate, and thus the most difficult, repair on a bike. Go easy at first, and try to be patient. Your spokes will appreciate it.

Removal of bottom bracket seal.

Cartridge bearings exposed.

Cone adjustments/wheel bearing maintenance —Finally, most cyclists are seldom out so long as to require wheel bearing service, and thus do not have to carry cone wrenches. ("Cones" are the threaded, cone-shaped pieces named for the tapering end which rests against the bearings; the other end is squared off to fit the wrench used to adjust pressure against the bearings.) Most of these mechanisms today are sealed, thus requiring no maintenance, and under normal conditions one needn't give one's cones a thought on tour. However, I pack the thin cone wrenches so that I can make the proper adjustments should anything go wrong on any of my rides, and of course when I pull full-bearing maintenance during winter cross-country tours.

Should you decide to readjust your cone bearing pressure, hold the lock-nut on one side of the hub (see drawing) with a crescent wrench or channel locks, and use a second wrench to loosen the locknut on the opposite hub side. Unscrew the lock nut completely, putting it somewhere so that you'll not kick it as you continue working. Next, remove the keyed lock washer ("keyed" refers to the small pointed flange of metal on the inside of the washer, which fits the groove on the axle). Now you can hold the locknut on the opposite hub side immobile, while very carefully adjusting cone pressure against the bearings on the dismantled side. As with so many adjustments on a bike, you are looking for that perfect point which allows free rotation of the wheel, but no lateral wheel sway.

When wishing to inspect or service (lube or replace) wheel bearings I usually remove the lock nut, keyed washer, and cone on one side of the axle only, and then carefully slide the axle out of the hub while watching for bearings that might fall out. In this manner I must rebuild only one side of the axle during reassembly.

The next task is getting past the seals. As already stated, most can be removed with a very thin knifeblade (a call to the shop where you bought your bike will tell you if you need a special tool, easily obtainable from SunTour), but you must take great care that they are not bent in the process. Just slip the blade in under the seal in various places around its perimeter and pry free.

Use the flat edge of your screwdriver to remove the bearings, but not until you have noticed two things—the very small gap which exists when all the bearings are present (they should not be wedged in tightly), and exactly how many bearings there are. If some bearings have fallen free when the axle was removed just count those and the bearings still in place and divide by two. You will then have the number you should replace on either side.

Now remove all the bearings, cleaning and inspecting each individually for pitting and cracks. Remember that bearings cost almost nothing compared to a hub; if you save a few cents by hanging on to worn-out bearings it will cost you a new hub in the end.

Bearing sizes generally fall into the following categories, but take one with you to the bike shop to make sure you buy proper replacements:

$\frac{3}{16}$"—front hub
$\frac{1}{4}$"—rear hub, bottom bracket
$\frac{1}{8}$"—freewheel
$\frac{5}{32}$"—pedal, headset

Once all bearings are removed and cleaned, wipe all grease out of the bearing races (the circular housing for the ball bearings). You are now ready to begin rebuilding the wheel.

Apply a bead of fresh grease to the bearing cup (race) of one side of the hub. Replace the bearings; then cover them with a second bead of grease. Replace the seal by laying it in place, then tapping lightly with the handle of your six-inch crescent wrench.

Take the axle (which still has the cone, lockwasher and lock nut on one side) and insert it into the hub side in which you have just replaced the bearings. Be sure to clean and check the cones for pitting as well, for they too are far less expensive to replace than an entire hub. Now you can turn your wheel over and replace the bearings in the other side, for the seal and cone will keep the bearings on the reverse side from falling out.

Once the bearings are in place around the axle on this second side, replace the seal, then thread the cone into place against the bearings only finger tight. Slide on the lockwasher and screw on the lock nut. Your hub is now rebuilt, but not ready to be ridden, for the cones have not been adjusted to the proper pressure against the bearings. Too loose, and the wheel will roll from side to side, in time ruining your bearings and cup and cone. Too tight, and the wheel will not roll easily.

Use the cone wrench to back off the cones a quarter turn or less if, when you turn the axle, it does not revolve easily in the hub. (The wheel is still off the bike; you should be checking its revolution by hand.) What usually happens is that a person will back off the cones too far, creating side-play. This is when the axle moves back and forth in the hub. Even a slight amount of movement will be greatly accentuated when the wheel is replaced on the frame, so try to remove the side-play while still retaining free rolling movement of the axle.

Cone wrench.

Just when you think you've got the best of both worlds, tighten the lock nuts on both sides. (Hold one side fast, with a crescent wrench or in a vise, while tightening the other side.) The first time you do this you will notice that you have tightened the cone somewhat by snugging the lock nuts—and you'll have to readjust the cone once more. Merely hold the lock nut on one side of the axle with your crescent wrench, while backing off the same-side cone ever so slightly with the cone wrench. This is usually sufficient to align it properly, but if not, back off the lock nut a quarter-turn and try again. Expect it to be difficult at first, and much easier the second time.

When side-play is absent and the axle moves freely, replace the axle washers and nuts (or quick-release mechanism) and restore the wheel to the frame. Once it is secured, spin the wheel and check again for rolling ease and for side-play. If it is not correct, do not sell your bicycle. Yell or kick the dog, and then return to your bike and adjust the cones once more. But don't give up.

Freewheel disassembly —Friction produced by the meeting of metal chain and metal freewheel sprocket teeth will at last wear them away so badly that they require replacement. The life of a sprocket can be extended greatly by correct alignment when changing gears; that is, train your ear to hear the noise produced when you haven't shifted the chain exactly over the cog. When you are way off center (sometimes spoken of as being "between gears") the clatter is unmistakable, but damage is being done even when the misalignment (and resultant noise) is much reduced but still present.

Sprocket life is also shortened by "cross-chaining"—a reference to the visual appearance when one's chain is forced onto the largest chainring and largest freewheel sprocket, or conversely upon the smallest chainring and smallest freewheel sprocket. Looking at either of these conditions from above shows the chain reaching at an awkward angle from the far inside of the chainrings to the far outside of the freewheel, or vice versa. In both instances the chain is stretched "across" the widths of chainring and freewheel, the angled metal edges eating away at chain links and sprocket teeth.

Proper shifting will give you very long sprocket life, but at some point one or two of them (those sprockets you use most often) will let you know they're getting old. Your chain will "skip" under pressure, a condition reversible only by sprocket replacement. Some riders erroneously believe they need a new freewheel at this time, a needlessly costly response. Simply invest in a couple sprocket tools (which you will need anyway for altering gear ratios), head to the shop for new sprockets (with the necessary information of type of freewheel and exact number of teeth), and learn the following repair procedure.

Because most of us do not have large workroom vises, I will describe the procedure of leaving the freewheel on the wheel and using two sprocket tools. If you do have a vise, place a slat of wood on either vise face to grip the largest sprocket, and close tightly. This in effect serves the purpose of a second

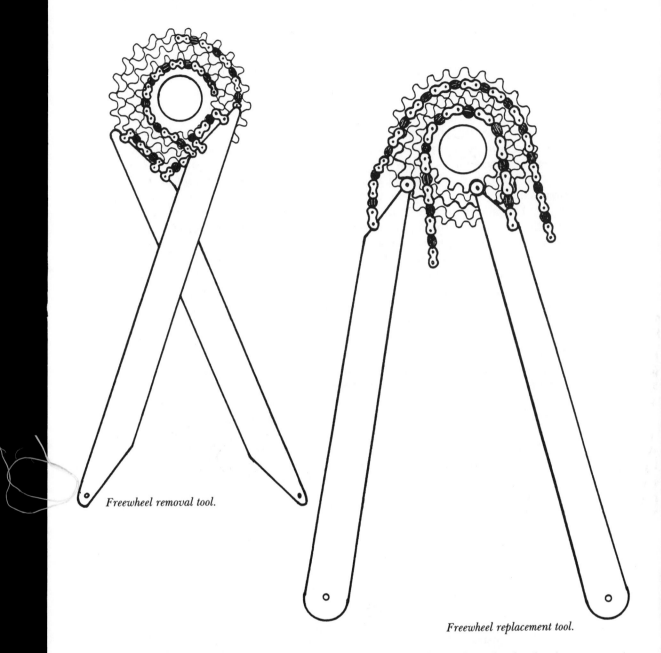

Freewheel removal tool.

Freewheel replacement tool.

sprocket tool. There are also commercial sprocket holders ("freewheel-axle vise tools") which take the place of the wood blocks and hold the cluster (freewheel) in a horizontal position for the easiest of all disassemblies.

When using two sprocket tools, place the chain of one tool around the fourth sprocket down (second to largest), wrapping the chain in a clockwise direction. Notice that the tools have a device (on the same rod end as the chain, but opposite side) to engage the sprocket and hold fast between the teeth; this device should be engaged and pointed in the direction you wish to turn that particular sprocket.

(A second and somewhat newer kind of sprocket tool is also available. In place of a rivet tip, this tool has a short length of chain, plus the longer one. The grip is more secure, the handles are crossed and pushed toward one another for disassembly. Follow the directions which come with these tools.)

In the opposite direction wrap the chain of the second tool around the first (smallest) cog. Place these tools so that the handles are only a few inches apart. This allows greater control, for the handles must be pushed toward one another to unscrew the top sprocket. A strong rider's freewheel will require a great deal of strength to disassemble, for the first two sprockets are actually tightened on the freewheel body during pedaling. (When you use two sprocket tools, be very careful not to apply uneven pressure against the handles, for this will cause the entire freewheel to tilt and your tools will slip off. No real problem, but it does propel one's knuckles into the sprocket teeth.)

On most freewheels the first two sprockets screw off the freewheel body or core in a counterclockwise direction, and the remaining cogwheels lift off. These last three have small lugs which fit the notches in the core, and usually have spacer rings between them. Don't get the sequence mixed up when you take things apart (I lay out each piece on newspaper as it comes off). Also, you *must* replace the sprockets with the same side up as you found them. If you drop one or get confused, study the bevel on the remaining cogs and match the errant sprocket accordingly.

Shimano cassette-type freewheels are broken down somewhat differently. The first sprocket or two will be removed in the same manner, but after that you will find several long, very thin bolts which reach through the inside perimeter of the remaining sprockets. Hold the top end of the bolt with a wrench, then reach around to the bottom with a second and unscrew the holding nuts. Now simply lift each sprocket free.

DERAILLEURS

Derailler in French means "to take from the rails"; in cycling it refers to the movement of one's chain from one sprocket to another. This is accomplished through a series of shifters, gear cables, and front and rear derailleurs.

Basically, a gear cable runs from the shifter (also called shift lever, shift handle or gear handle), along the down tube and chainstay, through a cable adjusting barrel (similar in principle to that found on brakes), to a cable clamp bolt on the changer (another name for derailleur). When you pull back on the shift lever (or push forward on a mountain bike's thumb shifter) you tighten the cable, which causes the derailleur to lift the chain from a smaller sprocket, and set it upon a larger one. Naturally, there are limits to how far in either direction you would wish your chain to go; this limitation is established by "high" and "low" gear adjusting screws. The high gear screw on rear derailleurs keeps the chain from moving beyond the smallest sprocket and falling off the freewheel; the low gear screw keeps the chain from moving beyond the largest sprocket and attacking your spokes. The third screw present on some changers is an "angle" screw. Chains, like cables, stretch over time, and thereby change the angle of the derailleur and thus its performance. This angle screw allows for taking up this tiny bit of slack, by resetting the proper angle in relation to the freewheel.

Below the derailleur housing are two pulleys, or rollers. Notice that the chain rolls over one and under the scond. The top pulley is the "jockey" or "guide" pulley—named for its job of jockeying the chain into place over a sprocket. The bottom one is the "tension" pulley, for it takes up the slack in the chain when the derailleur moves from a larger to a smaller sprocket. The final thing you should notice are the points of lubrication—small holes in the derailleur body which run toward the internal springs. Apply a couple drops of oil each month, and wipe off the excess.

Derailleur adjustment —Once again it is necessary to remind ourselves that everything on a bike is mechanical and understandable, not magic. For some reason riders appear to dread touching their derailleurs, and thus needlessly put up with inexact gear changes, dropped chains, and an inability to shift into particular gears.

By far the most frequent "transmission" problem encountered by cyclists can be solved with a few slight turns of the "high" and "low" gear adjusting screws. Let's say your chain can't quite make it up onto the largest sprocket of

Set screws for rear derailleur (notice "L" and "H" for low and high).

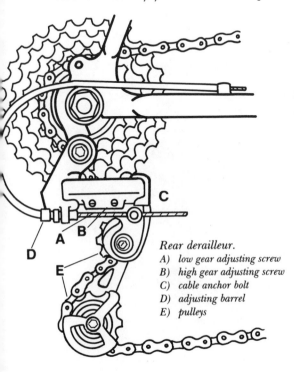

Rear derailleur.
A) low gear adjusting screw
B) high gear adjusting screw
C) cable anchor bolt
D) adjusting barrel
E) pulleys

the freewheel. Recalling that the larger freewheel sprockets provide the lower (easier to pedal) gears, simply turn counterclockwise the "L" screw of the rear derailleur—a quarter- or half-turn to start. If your chain falls off the smallest sprocket (highest gear) of your freewheel, turn the "H" screw on the rear derailleur clockwise—thereby limiting the chain's movement away from the freewheel.

Similar problems with the chainrings in front can be solved through the adjustment of the front derailleur limiting screws. Look closely inside the derailleur housing and you'll be able actually to see these limiting screws making contact with the body.

Let's go back to the problem of the chain not quite reaching up onto the largest freewheel sprocket. You've adjusted the "L" screw, can in fact see that the housing is not making contact with this limiting screw, and yet the chain can't quite fall into place. In such a case (very infrequent) the problem is not with the derailleur, but with the cable. It has stretched over time, and now must be readjusted. Most recent bikes have gear cable adjustment barrels to remove this slack quickly and easily (as with the brake cable adjustment systems); if yours does not you'll have to loosen the "cable fixing bolt" (which clamps the cable into place on the derailleur housing), shorten the cable slightly, and then tighten the fixing bolt again.

Cable replacement —Today's cables break very infrequently, but you

Front derailleur.
A) *low gear adjusting screw*
B) *high gear adjusting screw*
C) *cage*
D) *cable anchor bolt*

Front derailleur set screws.

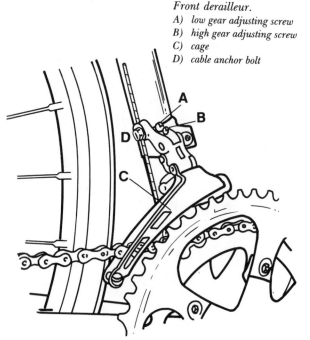

must know how to replace one. Otherwise, if it's the rear cable (as it almost always is due to its far more frequent use) you'll have to pedal all the way home in your hardest gear.

Begin by loosening the cable fixing bolt of whichever derailleur is affected by the broken cable. Remove the cable. (If the rear derailleur is involved, screw the cable adjusting barrel clockwise—into the derailleur body—until it stops.) Next, move to the other end of the cable and begin the very careful dismantling of your gear shift lever assembly. I always lay out the pieces in the same sequence as they are removed, so that I won't be racked by indecision over which piece comes next when I'm rebuilding it. Remove the lever fixing bolt (most recent models have a bale device on top) and cover, install a new cable (cutting off the unnecessary end, as you did with the brake cable), then replace the cover and fixing bolt. Place the lever in its most relaxed (no tension being applied to the cable) position. Feed the new cable through the cable housing. (I grease mine slightly before doing this), then through the cable adjusting barrel (on rear derailleurs), and on to the cable fixing bolt.

When replacing a rear derailleur cable, place the chain on the smallest front chainring. Pull the cable slightly taut (not so much that the derailleur body moves) and secure it by tightening the cable fixing bolt. The rear derailleur pulleys should be in line with the smallest freewheel sprocket at this point. If they are not, turn the high gear adjusting screw until that line is attained; if it cannot be reached with the adjusting screw it means you have pulled the cable too tight. Loosen the cable fixing bolt and readjust the cable tension.

To make the low gear adjustment, carefully shift the chain onto the largest freewheel sprocket; if this can't be done, turn the low gear adjusting screw counterclockwise until it can. Then adjust the thumb shifter until the rear derailleur pulleys are in perfect line with the largest freewheel sprocket, and turn the low gear adjusting screw clockwise—into the changer body—until you feel resistance.

When replacing a front derailleur cable, place the chain on the largest rear and smallest front sprockets. Then turn the low gear adjusting screw until there's a slight clearance between the chain and the inside plate of the chain cage (chain guide). If this cannot be done it means you have pulled the cable too taut; loosen the cable anchor bolt, correct the tension, and re-tighten.

Next, place the chain on the smallest rear and largest front sprockets. Then turn the high gear adjusting screw until there is a slight clearance between the chain and the outside plate of the chain cage. When these adjustments to the rear and front derailleurs have been made, switch the chain through all possible gear combinations. In each gear you should be able to position the derailleurs so that the chain does not make noise and does not rub against the metal inner and outer plates.

■Assembly and Adjustment

1. Assembly to Frame

Secure the bracket axle to the rear dropout with a 6mm hexagon wrench.

Note: When installing, be careful that the B-tension adjustment bolt is not deformed by coming into contact with the dropout tab.

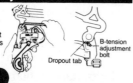

B-tension adjustment bolt

Dropout tab

2. Chain Assembly

Put the chain on the largest front chainwheel and the largest rear sprocket of the freewheel. Stretch the chain to the limit and add 2 chain links.

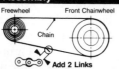

Freewheel   Front Chainwheel

Chain

Add 2 Links

3. Stroke adjustment and cable connection

•Stroke adjustment
Make adjustment of the derailleur stroke before making the SIS adjustment. At this time, make the adjustment with the lever in the friction mode.

SIS ➡ Friction system

1. Top adjustment
Turn the top adjustment bolt to adjust so that, looking from the rear, the guide pulley is below the outer line of the top gear. When the top adjustment bolt (H) is turned clockwise, it moves to the low side.

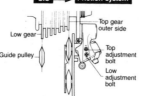

Low gear

Guide pulley

Top gear outer side

Top adjustment bolt

Low adjustment bolt

2. Inner cable connection
Connect the inner cable to the rear derailleur and, after the pre-stretch as shown in the figure, reset the cable to eliminate cable slack.

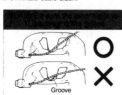

Pre-stretch the cable and remove its slack

Groove

O

X

3. Low adjustment
Turn the low adjustment bolt to adjust so that the guide pulley moves to a position directly below the low gear. When the low adjustment bolt (L) is turned clockwise, it moves to the top side.

4. How to use B-tension adjustment bolt

① Place the chain on the smallest chainwheel gear and the largest freewheel gear, and then turn the B-tension adjustment bolt to adjust so that the guide pulley moves to the position closest to the low gear.
② If the chain rubs when pedaling in reverse, the guide pulley is too close to the low gear. Turn B-tension adjustment bolt clockwise until the rubbing and noise disappear.

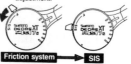

Set as close as possible.

Largest gear

Smallest gear

B-Tension adjustment bolt

Guide pulley

5. SIS adjustment

① Move the shifting lever from friction to SIS, and make the SIS adjustment.

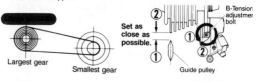

Friction system ➡ SIS

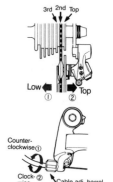

3rd 2nd Top

Low ⬅ ➡ Top

Counter-clockwise①

Clock-② wise ↘ Cable adj. barrel

② Operate the shifting lever to shift the chain from the top gear to the 2nd gear.
• If the chain will **not move to the 2nd gear**, turn the cable adjusting barrel to increase the tension.....① **(counter clockwise)**
• If the chain **moves past the 2nd gear**, decrease the tension..... ② **(clockwise)**

③ Next, with the chain on the 2nd gear, increase the inner cable tension while turning the crank forward. Stop turning the cable adjusting barrel **just before the chain makes noise against the 3rd gear**. This completes the adjustment.

Please note: Specifications are subject to change for improvement without notice.(English)

Courtesy Shimano

Shimano Index System (SIS) gear assembly and adjustment (Courtesy Shimano).

CHAIN

Beyond the occasional drop of oil after much wet weather, the thin-tire cyclist need not worry too much about his chain. But this is not the case for mountain bikers who live in mud. Beyond thorough cleanings, however, I have had only two very infrequent problems, no matter the abuse I give this portion of my transmission: frozen and broken links.

You'll need a chain rivet tool to free frozen links, and to add a new link if one breaks. Look at this tool very carefully while going through the following instructions.

Frozen and broken links —When a link becomes frozen (a condition often caused by insufficient lubrication) it makes itself known by jumping over the teeth in the sprockets, or by causing the rear derailleur to jerk forward suddenly as it passes over the jockey and tension pulleys. Elevate your rear wheel and turn the crank to find the culprit link, and when you do coat it with a light oil and work the link with your fingers. This may free it. If not, you'll have to employ the tool.

When viewed from the side, the chain tool looks like a wide "U," with two shorter "walls" of metal between. Place the tool in front of you with the handle to the right side. Twist the handle counterclockwise to remove the rivet "pin" from view. Now, take the chain and place it over the first of these inner walls from the right side. (It will usually be somewhat wider than the left-hand wall.) Notice, when you view your chain tool from the top, that these walls have an open space in the middle, and the chain roller rests in it with the "plates" on either side of the wall. (Look at an individual link. Each is made up of these metal side plates, small bars called "rollers" to engage the teeth of sprockets, and tiny rivets to hold the side plates and rollers together.)

To free a frozen link, place it as described above on the right-hand wall of the chain rivet tool. Turn the tool handle clockwise until the tool rivet pin touches the chain rivet. As you turn the handle more, notice how the plates move slightly farther apart. Most often only the slightest rivet adjustment is

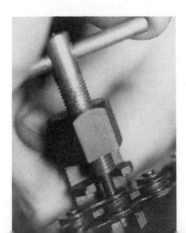

Chain rivet tool in action; notice rivet pin being pushed through the roller and side plate.

necessary to free the link. Be sure not to push the chain rivet flush with the side plate, for its length is such that it should extend slightly past the plates on both sides. If it is necessary to push the rivet flush to free the link, simply turn the chain over in the tool and apply pressure against the opposite end of the rivet.

In the case of a chain break, you must remove the broken link completely and replace it with a spare. This requires that the chain rivet be driven out of one side plate past the roller, yet still remaining in place in the far side plate. (I *know* this sounds very confusing. But it won't be when you're attempting the repair.) Keeping the rivet in the far side plate can be a little tricky at first, so I suggest you run through this procedure a couple times before a very long ride. Bike shops will often have lengths of old chains with which you can practice.

Place the chain over the left-hand wall of your chain tool, and turn the handle clockwise until the tool rivet pin touches the chain rivet. Then continue turning very carefully, until the roller can be pulled free, but with the chain rivet still in the far side plate. Install the new link by turning the chain tool around and driving the chain rivet through the new roller and side plate. You'll probably find that it's frozen when replaced. If so, simply place this link on the right-hand plate and free it, following the directions above.

Lubrication and cleaning —Try a single drop of oil on each roller, followed by a rubbing of the entire chain with a lightly oiled cloth. I then turn the cranks a few times and wait several minutes for the lubricant to penetrate past the rivets. Next, I wipe the chain with a dry cloth, for visible oil does nothing to minimize friction and merely attracts dust. Some of my fellow riders have had good luck on dirt roads and trails with "dri-lube" or other non-petroleum synthetic lubricants, as these attract less dirt. Others melt blocks of paraffin in a coffee can on the stove, and dip their perfectly clean, dry chains. It produces, for a while, a lubed, quiet, clean set of link that attracts no dirt whatsoever. I tried this a decade ago on a thin-tire bike, but decided against it because one cannot simply apply a bit of extra lubricant whenever necessary on the road.

For a quick cleaning while at home I use the Vetta Chain Cleaner, a plastic brush-and-solvent reservoir which mounts on the chain while it is in place on the bike. Should you have a muddy encounter on tour, however, you'll have no choice but to remove the chain, swish it about in a coffee can of kerosene or similar cleaner, and donate a toothbrush to the effort for particularly gummed-up areas.

After many thousands of miles you'll have to replace your old chain. (Worn-out chains have considerable lateral play, and will be somewhat noisy no matter the amount of lubricant.) At this time you'll probably find it necessary as well to replace the smallest two cogs of your freewheel, for these wear down more quickly than the other cogs, and thus are formed to the stretched-out links of your old chain.

When replacing a chain, count the number of links in your old one and install an exact duplicate. If, however, you for some reason are not sure how many links you should have, follow this procedure. It is not the easiest, but one of the more accurate.

Put your new chain on the largest sprockets front and rear. This should just about pull your rear derailleur cage until it is parallel with the chainstay. Give it some assistance by pulling the chain taut if needed, then lift the chain at the top of the chainring. You should have between one-half and one full link of extra chain at this point.

PEDALS

Sealed mountain bike pedals seldom require maintenance. But leave them a bit too long and you'll develop a squeak that you probably at first think is coming from your bottom bracket. This is when access to the bearings is a must.

Begin by removing the oval, outer pedal guard (not present on all models) with a very small allen wrench. A larger allen is then needed to remove the pedal spindle cap, which exposes the cone lock nut, lock washer, cone, and seal. Remove all, including the seal, in the same manner as described earlier in wheel bearing maintenance. (Except for cone removal, that is. Due to the pedal

ITEM NO.	DESCRIPTION
1	Cap
2	Pedal Axle Unit (Right/B.C.9/16"x20T.P.I.)
	Pedal Axle Unit (Right/UNF1/2"x20T.P.I.)
	Pedal Axle Unit (Left/B.C.9/16"x20T.P.I.)
	Pedal Axle Unit (Left/UNF1/2"x20T.P.I.)
3	Steel Ball (1/8") 10 pcs.
4	Seal
5	Plate Fixing Screw
6	Right Side Plate
	Left Side Plate
7	Toe-Clip Adapter (2 sets) Option

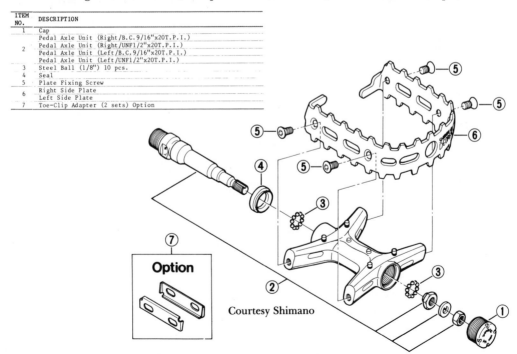

Option

Courtesy Shimano

housing a wrench cannot reach the cone. The cone therefore has slots cut into its side—the side facing you—for a screwdriver. Using a small screwdriver tip, simply back the cone off the spindle or pedal axle.)

Remove the cone, catching all bearings. Slip off the pedal, clean, inspect, and lubricate the bearings, bearing cups, and cones on both sides.

Reassemble. Adjust the cone for proper pressure against the bearings in the same manner as described in wheel maintenance—free pedal rotation but no side-play.

Replace the outer pedal guard.

Maintenance can be pulled with the pedal on or off the bike, by the way. I prefer leaving it in place, but if you wish it removed you might require a specially made pedal wrench. Many mountain bike pedals now, however, can be reached with a common open-end wrench. (Even if you manage to fit your six-inch crescent wrench in place, do *not* use it to remove the pedal. The great torque required will ruin the slide mechanism of your wrench.)

BOTTOM BRACKETS

To avoid confusion I will mention once again the fact that several parts of a bike have more than one name. In this repair we have the crank assembly of chainwheels (chainrings), the cranks (crankarms), and bottom bracket spindle (axle).

Take a close look at the entire assembly. I usually pull maintenance on bottom bracket bearings without ever touching the right side of the system— the side with the chainrings. Why? Because it's far easier and faster to remove only the left-side crank, lock ring and adjustable cup, and take out the right side bearings by reaching through the short bottom bracket. I will, however, go through the steps necessary to remove all pieces, and you can decide for yourself how you wish to reach your bearings.

Chainring removal/disassembly —Begin by removing the two small plastic or metal crankarm dust caps, usually with a small allen wrench or screwdriver tip. The crankarm fixing bolts are now exposed. Universal tools have heads fitted for various sizes of bolts; crank tools made specifically for one type of crank will have one end which fits the crankarm bolt, and the other end beveled to accept the jaws of a larger crescent, or a short breaker bar assembly to twist off the bolt. Remove the crankarm bolt (let's assume we're working with the right-chainring side), and *don't* forget to remove the washer as well. Fail to pull out the washer and the next step will not work. (Crankarm bolts on both sides are removed counterclockwise.)

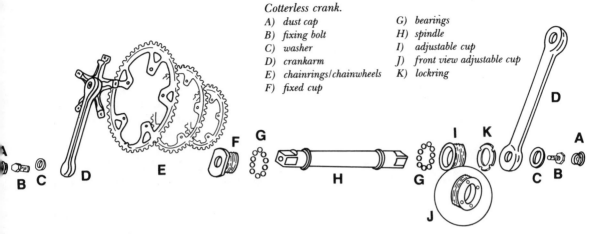

Cotterless crank.

A) *dust cap*
B) *fixing bolt*
C) *washer*
D) *crankarm*
E) *chainrings/chainwheels*
F) *fixed cup*
G) *bearings*
H) *spindle*
I) *adjustable cup*
J) *front view adjustable cup*
K) *lockring*

*Crankset closeup showing multi-piece crank,
cotterless crank dustcap, and smallest of three
chainrings.*

Cotterless crankbolt.

Screw the crankarm puller into the crankarm as far as it will go, making sure that the threads mesh perfectly.

Now insert the extractor portion—that piece which turns through the inside of the puller—into the puller body; turn it by hand until you feel its tip engage the spindle (axle) end. With a breaker bar, crescent or universal tool, turn the extractor; you will see the chainring assembly begin to slide toward you, away from and off the spindle. Lift the chain off the chainring, place it out of the way on the bottom bracket housing, and remove the left-side crankarm in the same manner.

This is an excellent time to clean your chainrings, check your pedals, and make sure the "chainring fixing bolts"—those which hold the sprockets together, located near the spider (the five metal arms radiating out from the crankarm to the attachment points for the chainrings)—are tight. (I usually check these for tightness every few weeks, without removing the chainrings from the bike to do so.) These seldom come loose, but if they do they'll produce an untrue chainring, and cause chain rub and noise on the front derailleur cage. The individual chainrings can be separated easily by using an allen wrench to remove these fixing bolts, and lifting off the rings.

Bottom bracket disassembly —Once the crankarms are removed, you can proceed to the bottom bracket. As I mentioned, I remove only the left side adjustable cup, but the fixed cup on the right (chainring) side can be removed with a lock ring/fixed cup tool—counterclockwise.

When out on the road or trail one can bang away with a screwdriver tip and flat side of a crescent to remove the lock ring and adjustable cup. But in time you'll destroy your lock ring this way; besides, you shouldn't need to mess with your bottom bracket when you're out unless you've been out for about a year, or under water for a week or so. Using the proper tool (the lock ring/fixed cup tool), engage the angled tip in the lock ring notch, and remove it—counterclockwise. Now use an adjustable cup tool to engage the "pin holes" in the cup's face, and back it out completely.

Remove the seal as described in the wheel bearing maintenance discussion earlier. The ball bearings will probably be in a retainer ring. If so, notice in which direction the retainer faces as you remove the spindle; the solid back of the retainer should face *away* from you. Also notice if one end of the spindle is longer than the other. If it is, the longer side will extend toward the chainrings. Clean, inspect, and if necessary, replace all bearings. Wipe all surfaces clean and inspect the spindle and cups for bearing wear.

Bottom bracket reassembly —Apply a generous bead of grease on the inside of your fixed cup, replace the bearings, and cover them with a second layer of grease. Now thread this cup back into the frame (right side, chainring

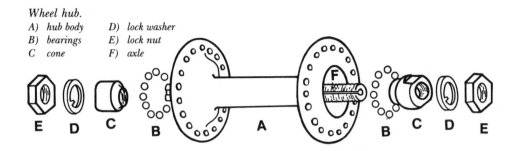

Wheel hub.

A) *hub body* D) *lock washer*
B) *bearings* E) *lock nut*
C *cone*   F) *axle*

E D C B A B C D E

side), snugging it well. To insure easy removal some months in the future, always apply a bit of grease to the threads inside the bottom bracket before replacing the cups. (Note that if you have not removed this fixed cup you will have to reach through the bottom bracket, and from the right side through the axle hole in the seal, to clean/lube/replace bearings.)

Lubricate and replace the bearings in the adjustable cup in the same manner, but do not yet thread the cup into place.

Take the cleaned spindle, longer side toward the fixed cup and, from the other side of the bike (left side) carefully guide it through the bracket and fixed cup.

While holding the spindle by one end, pick up the adjustable cup, engage the spindle in the cup hole, and thread it into the frame. Stop threading this cup when it engages the bearings, and check for side-play in the spindle. If it is present, thread the cup a bit further, but not so far as to prohibit the free turning of the spindle.

When the adjustment is correct replace the lock ring, then re-check for proper bearing adjustment. As with wheels, this can be troubling until you get the hang of it, for the lock ring can budge the adjustable cup a bit and throw you off. Have patience.

Replace both crankarms by slipping them onto the spindle, and tightening the fixing bolts. These must be well secured, and should be checked for tightness once every forty or fifty miles for the next two hundred miles. Re-engage the chain on the chainring, and you're ready to roll.

Postscript

By this point of the book you possess sufficient knowledge to choose, ride, and maintain a mountain bike for cross-town commutes, weekend jaunts, and around-the-world journeys. ATBs are as all-purpose as they are all-terrain, and one unexpected benefit I've learned to appreciate is that of linking up with fellow riders on organized mountain bike trips. The number of private-company offerings is great (as a glance at the back pages of any bike magazine will indicate), as are the national and even international settings one can choose to tour.

I have ridden with four such companies: Backroads Bicycle Touring, Backcountry Bicycle Tours, Rim Tours, and The Road Less Traveled. I also plan to ride with three others—Vermont Bicycle Touring, Kaibab Bike Tours, and Utah Outback (about which I have heard good things from fellow tourers whose opinions I trust)—this coming year. All have my hearty recommendations, and will provide you with the kind of personal attention, encouragement, instruction, and back-up services which make mountain bike touring for the first time—or the millionth—a delight. (Addresses in the Appendix.)

As mentioned earlier, I am on the road some six months each year. Like most people I enjoy receiving letters; unlike most, I have a wonderful excuse for not answering them quickly. But I promise that if you choose to drop a line—about the book if you wish, but preferably about your experiences while commuting, trail riding or touring—I will, ultimately, reply:

Dennis Coello
470 South 1300 East, #409
Salt Lake City, Utah 84102

It remains only for me to wish you good luck and safe cycling. All the best.

APPENDIX A: *Gear Chart for 26" Wheel*

Number of teeth in front sprocket

	24	26	28	30	32	34	36	38	40	42	44	46	48	50	52
12	52	56.3	60.7	65	69.3	73.4	78	82.3	86.7	91	95.3	99.7	104	108.3	112.7
13	48	52	56	60	64	68	72	76	80	84	88	92	96	100	104
14	44.6	48.3	52	55.8	59.4	63.1	66.9	70.6	74.3	78	81.7	85.4	89.1	92.9	96.6
15	41.6	45.1	48.5	52	55.5	58.9	62.4	65.9	69.3	72.8	76.3	79.7	83.2	86.7	90.1
16	39	42.3	45.5	48.8	52	55.3	58.5	61.8	65	68.3	71.5	74.8	78	81.3	84.5
17	36.7	39.8	42.8	45.9	48.9	52	55.1	58.1	61.2	64.2	67.3	70.4	73.4	76.5	79.5
18	34.7	37.6	40.4	43.3	46.2	49.1	52	54.9	57.8	60.7	63.6	66.4	69.3	72.2	75.1
19	32.8	35.6	38.3	41.1	43.8	46.5	49.3	52	54.7	57.8	60.2	62.9	65.7	68.4	71.2
20	31.2	33.8	36.4	39	41.6	44.2	46.8	49.4	52	54.6	57.2	59.8	62.4	65	67.6
21	29.7	32.2	34.7	37.1	39.6	42.1	44.6	47	49.5	52	54.5	57	59.4	61.9	63.4
22	28.4	30.7	33.1	35.5	37.8	40.2	42.5	44.9	47.3	49.6	52	54.4	56.7	59.1	61.5
23	27.1	29.4	31.7	33.9	36.2	38.4	40.7	43	45.2	47.5	49.7	52	54.3	56.5	58.8
24	26	28.2	30.3	32.5	34.7	36.8	39	41.2	43.3	45.5	47.7	49.8	52	54.2	56.3
25	25	27	29.1	31.2	33.3	35.4	37.4	39.5	41.6	43.7	45.8	47.8	49.9	52	54.1
26	24	26	28	30	32	34	36	38	40	42	44	46	48	50	52
27	23.1	25	27	28.9	30.8	32.7	34.7	36.6	38.5	40.4	42.4	44.3	46.2	48.1	50.1
28	22.3	24.1	26	27.9	29.7	31.6	33.4	35.3	37.1	39	40.9	42.7	44.6	46.4	48.3
29	21.5	23.3	25.1	26.9	28.7	30.5	32.3	34.1	35.9	37.7	39.4	41.2	43	44.8	46.6
30	20.8	22.5	24.3	26	27.7	29.5	31.2	32.9	34.7	36.4	38.1	39.9	41.6	43.3	45.1
31	20.1	21.8	23.5	25.2	26.8	28.5	30.2	31.9	33.5	35.2	36.9	38.6	40.3	41.9	43.6
32	19.5	21.1	22.8	24.4	26	27.6	29.3	30.9	32.5	34.1	35.8	37.4	39	40.6	42.3
33	18.9	20.5	22.1	23.6	25.2	26.7	28.4	29.9	31.5	33.1	34.7	36.2	37.8	39.4	41
34	18.4	19.9	21.4	22.9	24.5	26	27.5	29.1	30.6	32.1	33.6	35.2	36.7	38.2	39.8
35	17.8	19.3	20.8	22.3	23.8	25.3	26.7	28.2	29.7	31.2	32.7	34.2	35.7	37.1	38.6
36	17.3	18.8	20.2	21.7	23.1	24.6	26	27.4	28.9	30.3	31.8	33.2	34.7	36.1	37.6

Number of teeth in rear sprocket (row label, left side)

$$\text{inch gear} = \frac{\text{\# teeth in front sprocket}}{\text{\# teeth in rear sprocket}} \times \text{wheel diameter in inches}$$

Example: $\frac{48}{13} \times 26 = 96$ inch gear

(Compute linear distance traveled with each crank rotation by multiplying "inch gear" by pi = 3.14)

Example: $96 \times 3.14 = 301.44''$ (or 25.12′ linear distance)

Some people contend that the higher profile tires on 26" mountain bike wheels makes them virtually the same, as far as gear ratios are concerned, as 27" thin tires. I have measured the difference, computed it over the length of several day rides or a single weekend tour, and cannot agree.

APPENDIX B: *Bicycle Organizations*

National Off-Road Bicycle Association
(NORBA)
P.O. Box 1901
Chandler, AZ 85244
(602) 961-0635

League of American Wheelmen
(LAW)
Suite 209
6707 Whitestone Road
Baltimore, MD 21207
(301) 944-3399

Bikecentennial
P.O. Box 8308
Missoula, MT 59807
(406) 721-1776

International Mountain Bicycling
Association (IMBA)
Route 2 Box 303
Bishop, CA 93514
(619) 387-2757

American Trails
1400 Sixteenth Street N.W.
Suite 300
Washington, DC 20036
(202) 797-5418

Canadian Cycling Association
333 River Rd.
Vanier, Ont. K1L 8B9
CANADA
(613) 748-5629

Great Canadian Bicycle Rally
Box 245
Paris, Ont. N3L 2C9
CANADA
(519) 442-6235

New Brunswick Cycling Association
131 Sussex Ave.
Riverview, N.B. E1B 3A5
CANADA

Ontario Cycling Association
1220 Sheppard Ave. East, Suite 216
Willowdale, Ont. M2K 2X1
CANADA
(416) 495-4141

Vancouver Bicycle Club
3541 W. 20th Ave.
Vancouver, B.C. V6S 1E6
CANADA

In Canada

Bicycling Association of B.C.
332 1367 W. Broadway
Vancouver, B.C. V6H 4A9
CANADA
(604) 737-3034

APPENDIX C: *Bike Magazines*

BICYCLE USA
(magazine for LAW members)
Suite 209
6707 Whitestone Road
Baltimore, MD 21207

BICYCLE GUIDE
711 Boylston Street
Boston, MA 02116

BICYCLING
33 East Minor Street
Emmaus, PA 18049

CYCLIST
20816 Higgins Court
Torrance, CA 90501

FAT TIRE FLYER
P.O. Box 757
Fairfax, CA 94930

MOUNTAIN BIKE
33 East Minor Street
Emmaus, PA 18049

MOUNTAIN BIKING
10968 Via Frontera
San Diego, CA 92127

MOUNTAIN BIKE ACTION
P.O. Box 9502
Mission Hills, CA 91345-9502

APPENDIX D: *Pannier Companies*

Cannondale
9 Brookside Place
Georgetown, CT 06829

Eclipse
P.O. Box 7370
Ann Arbor, MI 48107

Kangaroo Baggs
3891 North Ventura Avenue
Ventura, CA 93001

Kirtland
P.O. Box 4059
Boulder, CO 80306

Lone Peak
3474 South 2300 East
Salt Lake City, UT 84109

Madden USA
2400 Central Avenue
Dept. MB4
Boulder, CO 80301

Robert Beckman Designs
(formerly Needle Works)
P.O. Box 6952
Bend, OR 97708

Note: This is not intended as an inclusive list of all pannier manufacturers, but instead as help in beginning the process of searching for the right saddlebags for your biking style and budget. As suggested in the text, any bike magazine will contain advertisements for additional companies.

The following are two of the rack companies mentioned in the text; again, there are several other brands available through bike shops and catalogues.

Blackburn   Bruce Gordon Cycles
75 Cristich Lane   221-C Water Street
Campbell, CA 95008   Petaluma, CA 94952

APPENDIX E: *Federal Land Information*

The information provided in Chapter 6, plus your state and local offices, should make it clear which areas are off-limits to mountain-bike travel. For further information contact NORBA (address in Appendix B), or write to the following offices:

BUREAU OF LAND MANAGEMENT (BLM)
U.S. Department of the Interior
18th and "C" Streets, N.W.
Room 1013
Washington, D.C. 20240

NATIONAL FORESTS AND WILDERNESS AREAS
Forest Service
U.S. Department of Agriculture
12th and Independence Streets, S.W.
P.O. Box 2417
Washington, D.C. 20013

NATIONAL PARKS AND RELATED AREAS
National Park Service
U.S. Department of the Interior
18th and "C" Streets, N.W.
Room 1013
Washington, D.C. 20240

APPENDIX F: *Touring Companies*

A complete list of bicycle touring companies would require many pages; you will find names and addresses in the back pages of most cycling magazines. The following are the companies with which I've toured, plus Vermont Bicycle Touring, Kaibab Bike Tours, and Utah Outback.

BACKCOUNTRY BICYCLE TOURS
P.O. Box 4029
Bozeman, MT 59715
(406) 586-3556

BACKROADS BICYCLE TOURING
P.O. Box 1626
San Leandro, CA 94577
(415) 895-1783

KAIBAB BIKE TOURS
395 South 600 East
Salt Lake City, UT 84102
(801) 649-9087

RIM TOURS
94 West 1st North
Moab, UT 84532
(801) 259-5223

THE ROAD LESS TRAVELED
P.O. Box 39
West Yellowstone, MT 59758

UTAH OUTBACK
P.O. Box 1171
Salt Lake City, UT 84110
(801) 583-8929

VERMONT BICYCLE TOURING
Box 711
Bristol, VT 05443
(802) 453-4811

APPENDIX G: *Miscellaneous Cycle Products*

The Bike Slider (bike rack)
1435 Gardena Avenue
Suite 12
Glendale, CA 91204
(800) 522-SLDR
(800) 822-7537 (in California)

Kroop's Goggles, Inc.
9865-E North Washington Blvd.
Laurel, MD 20707
(301) 498-5848

The LeGuard Company
1410 Ash Drive
Bozeman, MT 59715
(406) 587-1115

Mountain Aid Products (kickstand)
Department C
P.O. Box 44
San Clemente, CA 92672
(714) 492-5875

Mountain Tamer Quad
(fourth chainring)
P.O. Box 53426
Albuquerque, NM 87153-3426
(505) 294-3368

Paul's Cycle Sacs (available in
   some bike shops, but if you
   have difficulty in
   locating, write to:)
105 Bennett Avenue
#33A
New York, NY 10033
(212) 795-3421

Roly Pearson (Roly caps)
730 West 400 North
Salt Lake City, UT 84116
(801) 539-8475

Wasatch Touring (Seat Leash)
702 East 100 South
Salt Lake City, UT 84102
(801) 359-9361

Wiggy's Inc. (sleeping bags)
P.O. Box 2124
Grand Junction, CO 81502
(303) 241-6465

Wild Side Designs (bike rack)
Department C
P.O. Box 621
Beaverton, OR 97075
(503) 649-9085

METRIC CONVERSION TABLE

1 inch = 2.54 centimetres
1 foot = 30 centimetres
1 yard = 91 centimetres
1 mile = 1.61 kilometres

Index